DON'T GO THERE

DON'T GO THERE

MARTIN 'JIM' McFADDEN

"A true and stark personal
account of one man's battle
with the bottle and his demons"

©Martin 'Jim' McFadden 2014
All rights reserved
www.martinjimmcfadden.com

CreateSpace Edition 2017

Designed by Jane Stark
Typeset in Adobe Caslon Pro
seamistgraphics@gmail.com

ISBN: 9781546327615

Printed and bound in Spain
by GraphyCems, Villatuerta, Navarra

This book is dedicated to my wife Liz,
whom I love very much.

In memory of my father James McFadden
who died on 20th March 1993

My mother Sadie McFadden
who died on 8th October 1998

Love you Daddy and Mammy

May You Rest in Peace

I thank God for having such good parents, especially for so long.
You were always there for me especially when I needed you most.
Despite my challenging character and wild ways
you loved me just as I was,
and gave me the support I needed during the dark times.
You are my inspiration and I will always love you.

Also in memory of
my nephew Joseph McFadden,
who died 23rd May 1998

My brother Edmund,
who died 5th September 2005

Love you Joseph and Edmund

May You Rest in Peace

ACKNOWLEDGEMENTS

If my wife Liz hadn't come into my life when she did, I have no doubt I wouldn't have survived the battle ahead. I want to thank Liz for supporting and having faith in me, and for understanding my restless and unpredictable character as I battled to remain sober. I was only a very short time without a drink when I first met Liz, so I was at a very vulnerable stage of my life. With my chronic alcoholism, and reckless personality I sure was a high risk character, and nobody could have blamed Liz had she decided to walk away when I fell off the wagon for the first time.

I love you Liz, you are my everything xxx

I would also like to acknowledge and thank the Marian Fathers of the Immaculate Conception of the B.V.M. for their approval and permission to use a passage from the Diary of St Maria Faustina Kowalska: Divine Mercy in My Soul.

Marian Fathers of the Immaculate Conception of the B.V.M.

Copyright Office
Association of Marian Helpers

(Diary, 741) Diary of St Maria Faustina Kowalska:
Divine Mercy in My Soul © 1987 Marian Fathers
of the Immaculate Conception of the B.V.M.
Stockbridge, Mass 01263

My appreciation also goes to Fr Jose Maniyangat for giving me his approval and permission to share his own personal testimony.

When I decided to take my personal journey and to give an honest account of my life, especially through the darker years, I had much support from my family and friends. To my sisters Mary Teresa and Bridie and my brother Eunan and his wife Nancy, and all my nephews and nieces, thank you all for your patience, kindness and love during my wild times! Without your support I don't think I'd be here today.

To all my mates with whom I had the craic, thanks for all the laughs, during the highs and lows.

I would also like to take this opportunity to apologise sincerely to anyone, and everyone whom I might have offended or hurt with my words or actions during my earlier years of reckless behaviour, and the destruction and mayhem that followed as a result of my alcoholism. I am sober writing this today and have such a good quality of life that I would not have imagined it was possible some short years previously.

I would like this book to be an inspiration to anyone who is suffering from an addiction of any sort, and also to anyone who has a dream and doesn't have the confidence to follow and try to achieve that dream. I was and will always be a chronic alcoholic, and as you will also learn, my only form of education was some short years at national school when I was at such a young age I had no interest in learning, and didn't want to be there in the first place.

The stories told in this book are true and correct. However I have changed the names of some people to protect their identity.

I didn't have a camera,
So photos they were few,
But whatever I can remember,
I would like to share it here with you.

Martin 'Jim' McFadden

FOREWORD

I would like to acknowledge and thank Bishop Seamus Hegarty, retired Bishop of Derry for taking the time to read and approve my manuscript and for the following foreword.

When Martin 'Jim' McFadden requested me to "look through" the contents of his book which he was writing, little did I know when I agreed to do so that I was given access to a document of a personal profile of the author Martin 'Jim' McFadden.

It is a substantial account of the life of one who had more than a few escapades at home and abroad. The good news is that he survived many years in England by his capacity to defend and protect himself and his trust in God's love.

This book, a candid account of Martin Jim's life in England for many years.

Fortunately, Liz, his wife, was his support and inspiration. To comment further on any of my observations are a waste of space. Read Martin Jim's own book. It is fascinating and thrilling. I enjoyed the book very much. I commend it highly to readers. I hope you enjoy it as much as I did.

+ Séamus Hegarty,
Retired Bishop of Derry.

CONTENTS

PROLOGUE: Where It All Began 13

BOOK ONE: The Beginning of the Madness 15
Dom Doherty 39
Working for the County Council 40
My Nightmare Begins 42
My Accident 49
My First Time Out of Ireland 61
My Life of Mayhem Continues 68
Going to London 72
My Horrors on a Jet Plane 91
Going Back to London 97
My £90,000 Compensation 113
Meeting Karen 116
Continuing to Live Life on the Edge 126
Going to America 135
Going to Glasgow 141
Well and Truly Beat 145
The Death of my Father 147
Appendix – Book One 153

BOOK TWO: My Recovery 156
Meeting Liz 165
Starting Work in Letterkenny General Hospital 169

Mammy's Stroke and Eventual Death 173
Going Home Alone 175
Liz Joins Me in Carrigart 177
Our Wedding 180
Becoming Very Unsettled In Life 184
Drinking Again 186
The Death of My Brother Edmund 194
Hopefully My Last Drink 198

BOOK THREE: My Spiritual Journey Begins 200
    St Anthony 201
    St Anthony's Nine Tuesday Novena 205
Receiving My Rosary for the Third Time 210
My Spiritual Journey Continues 213
Our Guardian Angels 216
The Passing of Two Great Men 217
Searching For My Roots 219
My Devotion to the Holy Souls 224
Fr Jose Maniyangat 225
Church Dedicated to the Holy Souls in Purgatory . . 232
St Faustina's Vision of Hell 233
The Chaplet of Divine Mercy 235
Taking Stock of my Life 237

PROLOGUE

Where It All Began

"They took it from the Jims," my father would say. My mother, meanwhile, would reply by saying, "We all know who the Jims are and where they came from, but nobody seems to know who or where your family came from". That was an exchange of conversation my parents had on several occasions after the Guards called to our house looking for us for whatever reason.

— BOOK ONE —

The Beginning of the Madness

I was born in 1963 in the house which is still my home today. My father, James McFadden, was from Cashel, Creeslough, and my mother, Sadie McLaughlin, was from Dunmore, Carrigart. I was the youngest of five siblings. I had two brothers and two sisters. Edmund was the eldest, next came Mary Teresa, then Eunan and Bridie. I was always referred to as the baby or 'the wane' (short for wee one). Although I was actually baptised as John Martin McFadden, from the very beginning I was just referred to as Martin, in order to differentiate between myself and my uncle Johnny (mom's brother). As a result, my baptismal name John would only be used later during the process of filling out official documents, passport, driving license etc and I would become known locally as Martin 'Jim'.

I'm not sure how old I was when my mother took me to a holy well known locally as Doon Well. For some reason my hair still hadn't started to grow so my mother bathed my head in the well. After our visit my hair started growing. I do remember a few years later getting ringworm in my hair, but thankfully I also got cured from it.

From an early age my mother remained during the day at her former home caring for her own mother Sarah, and her brother Johnny. My grandmother Sarah had her leg amputated and my uncle Johnny was disabled due to suffering a brain haemorrhage at a young age. As their demands increased my mother also started staying overnight, so as a family we were sort of torn between two homes. For some reason I remained at home with my father. It always was a very special and peaceful home.

Later it was just the two of us together in our home at night. We didn't want or need a TV or any other of the mod cons so I suppose my childhood was slightly different to the mates I used to hang out and play with. They would all be talking about the previous night's TV viewing and even though I couldn't relate to that I didn't give a damn. I do remember, however, on Sunday nights, Daddy and myself would visit a neighbour's house. This house was equipped with a TV and we would all watch *The Riordan's*. Then I would have to sit while they all listened to the *News at Nine* and, to make matters worse, they would all remained glued to the *News at Ten* before finally switching off the TV.

We would also go to visit the same household when a world title boxing fight was taking place. Mohammed Ali was the man back then and I remember when Daddy and myself would be walking home I would be dancing on the roadway and swinging all sorts of punches, imagining myself knocking out various characters, including my teacher.

There is a small river close to our home and I got into the habit of walking across the top of the bridge, imagining I was some sort of a stunt man. We had a family dog that used to follow me everywhere and I remember he would sit happily waiting for me. One particular day, as I was doing my bridge walk, 'Spot' must have decided to join me and raced in between my legs, thus toppling me over. I remember somersaulting as I fell down into the river.

My next memory is waking up in the stream of water with my clothes soaked. I do not recall how long I had been laying there. I was uninjured. Had there been a heavy rain fall I would have most likely drowned as a result. I picked myself up and made my escape through our neighbour's garden. I remember crying as I raced home, fearful that anyone should see me in my distressed state.

The Beginning of the Madness

My memories of national school are not happy ones. At that time it was acceptable for teachers to slap their pupils and from my own memory some of them abused the system. I'm surprised today that none of them have been summoned to appear in front of a tribunal of some sort with a case to answer.

I remember one day our teacher had brought in a history book. He asked us to pass it around, and to be careful and not soil or bend the pages. When it arrived at our desk I knew my mate Sean was up to something as he was smiling to himself. He had the book open at a page showing a photograph of Patrick Pearse being questioned by two policemen. Mr Pearse had his hands folded behind his back, and Sean then got his biro and drew a revolver into his hand. We then tried to pass it onto the seat in front of us, but the two lads sensed something was wrong, and they threw it back to us.

This procedure was repeated several times before our teacher discovered what was happening. When he saw my mate's work of art he went into a rage that had him frothing at the mouth. He demanded to know who the culprit was, and although I wasn't looking forward to a thumping for something I didn't do, I knew I couldn't grass on my mate. Our teacher punished us both equally with six lashes of his cane, and although our hands were hot and sore for some time afterwards, we still laughed about it all.

We didn't play much football on our breaks. Instead we played marbles, hounds and hares, and rounders. Most of the time we would just wrestle with each other but it usually got out of hand.

In my final year at national school I was admitted to hospital to have my appendix removed. It was Christmas Eve. I remember the nurse asking me if I believed in Santa, to which I replied, "Yes". I knew by giving that answer I would get a present.

I had my operation that night and when I awoke early Christmas morning, Santa had delivered. I got a colouring book, crayons, and two comics, the *Dandy* and *Beano*. I really appreciated it, even though

I knew the score on Santa. I always loved Christmas as a child. We were always so excited on Christmas Eve, eagerly awaiting the visit of our friend. We really treasured the presents he brought us. I'm grateful for all those special memories.

Prayer played a big part in both our homes and we recited the Rosary each day. I remember my father would always go down on his knees first thing in the morning and say his prayers; he would repeat this same ritual last thing before retiring to bed. Whenever I made my way up to my mother's house she would always capture me to recite the Rosary with her, and if a neighbour or visitor came in they would usually kneel down and join in.

I remember whenever we got new clothes, Daddy would suggest we wear them for the first time when we went to Mass. Daddy would wear his best outfit and would polish his shoes every week before wearing them to Mass. When he returned home he would put them away neatly until the following Sunday.

We always went to Mass on a Sunday, but myself and my mates got into the habit of standing at the back of the church discussing the week's events. Quite often we were told to shut up by another Mass-goer, but that only made us worse and so we would just talk louder and make more noise. I remember one time challenging another lad to a fight outside the church door. Looking back now, I'm glad he didn't take me up on my offer.

I never finished my final year at national school and didn't sit the exams. That was the end of my education. I was thirteen years old. I never went to secondary school. I remember saying to my father, "It's only prigs that come out of there".

That same year I started my first job as a kitchen porter in our local hotel. The pay was £15 per week. I worked split shifts six days a week. The hours were 8am to 3pm and 5pm to 10pm. The work was hard. Most of the staff were crazy and the craic was good so I fitted in quite well.

I remember one time myself and the fellow working alongside me having a falling out with one of the cooks. We found out that when he sent his pots down to the pot wash for us to scrub they would be slightly burned, thus making it harder for us to clean them. A few days later, when we realised it wasn't just an accident, we decided on an easy way out of it. Instead of taking time to wash the pots we started dumping them in the rubbish bins. It wasn't long before there was a scarcity of pots and a big inquiry into what was happening to them. An old gentleman who had worked at the hotel from an early age lived there permanently in an adjoining house as a sort of a caretaker/friend of the family. Although he was retired he was always sniffing about and keeping an eye on events. He went to the compound where the rubbish was dumped and opened all the rubbish bags, and recovered every pot. I was shocked when he carried them all into the kitchen and ordered us to wash each one. Although they couldn't prove who dumped them, I knew from his knowing grin that he considered us guilty.

As there were a large number of people employed at the hotel, quite a few of whom were around my own age, there was always some sort of mischief afoot. The management were kept busy trying to control us. Sometimes they would have no option but to sack the dossers. I saw quite a few of my work colleagues 'walk the line' before it eventually came to my own turn some seasons later.

As there were also a lot of girls working there, I'm pretty sure there was plenty of romancing going on, but at that stage in my life I was more interested in playing a prank on my female work colleagues, rather than seeking a date with any of them.

I remember one day a girl sneaked up behind me and jumped up on my back. I don't know what her motive was, but we happened to be outside the manager's office. Instead of me carrying her off to someplace more private, I bent over and she fell over my head onto the floor. She managed to pull me down on top of her, and as I was trying to get free from her clutches, the manager, hearing the commotion, stormed out of his office. When he was angry or excited he had a habit of mixing up his words. As I was lying on top of my lady friend, the manager shouted "Youse are worse than two sex mechanics!" He wrongly assumed I was just about to lose my virginity, and in his confusion he meant to say we were worse than two sex maniacs.

Myself and the lads of my own age would spend our breaks just messing about down in the village. Earlier, in the hotel, we could have been fighting, and several times these fights would continue down the street. One of the shops had a large basket outside containing a number of footballs, and we used to take one for a kick about with the intention of returning it. During the summer it was usually quite busy, and I'm sure we annoyed a lot of people. One day, however, our new pastime came to a sudden end when one of us kicked the ball into the local chemist and smashed some expensive pottery in the process. The lady who owned the chemist refused to give us back the football until we had paid for the damage, so as we didn't have any money we decided to walk away and hope for the best. Thankfully, we didn't hear any more about that incident and we steered clear of both shops for a period afterwards.

On another occasion, myself and another fellow lifted our mate and placed him inside a shopping trolley and let him loose down the main street, at the mercy of oncoming traffic. The trolley came to a halt after it crashed into a wall and thank God our mate escaped uninjured.

That incident reminds me of a similar incident regarding my uncle Johnny, who was confined to a wheelchair. My cousin Denis and I, both aged about thirteen, took him out and were taking it in turns to push the chair. We had just reached the top of a hill and were breathless. Our uncle was a bit of a character and was slagging us about being unfit and useless. We then let go of the wheelchair with the good intention of catching it again before anything happened. However, it gathered speed so fast that it careered down the hill and we couldn't catch it. Our uncle was screaming and praying out aloud. We could only watch on helplessly as the chair hit the ditch, throwing Johnny headfirst into the hedge. Thank God he didn't suffer any serious injuries from that incident.

Another evening, Denis and I decided to build ourselves a go-kart. There were contractors building a house nearby and we managed to steal enough timber from it to build our frame. Then we decided to borrow the wheels from our uncle's wheelchair intending to replace them before the following morning. Our plans were short-lived, because on our third attempt at racing down a steep hill I lost control and crashed into a stone wall, thus smashing the two front wheels. I didn't sleep too well that night as I was worrying about confessing to Johnny, and felt guilty for leaving him housebound without his wheels.

During my first season working in the hotel I bought myself a bicycle. It was second-hand and cost me one week's wages. I also bought a large wall clock for my father's home. It was new and cost £15. That clock is still in good working condition and hangs in my hallway to this day.

The hotel season ended in September, after which it would remain closed until the following Easter. All of my mates had now started secondary school and I had a lot of time on my hands. When we met we would spend most of our time just walking or quite often being chased along the roads by angry car drivers, as we were usually up to some form of mischief.

One of us would stand along the road and hold out our hand in the hitching position, and the rest of the gang would hide behind the ditch. Whenever a car would stop the rest of us would scramble out over the hedge and all crowd into the car. This could end up in a real struggle, since the car often would have several passengers already on board.

Another prank was to hide behind hedges armed with raw eggs, and fire them at oncoming cars. We could be walking and running for miles, sometimes through dark fields and falling into ditches and drains. One night, I remember we borrowed a large white sheet from somebody's clothes line. We walked down to our local graveyard and took up position. When we saw a car approaching one of us stood in the middle of the road, with the sheet draped over his body, both hands outstretched and moving up and down. We were having great fun at that until finally the Gardai arrived in an unmarked car and gave chase. We all ran off through the fields in different directions. I remember approaching a dead end with a thick hawthorn hedge in front of me. I could hear the Garda saying "We have you now". I covered my face with my hands and dived right into the hedge and hoped for the best. I ripped my clothes in the process as I crashed through it, but did manage to make my escape unharmed. We enjoyed the chase so much that we used to go robbing apples from orchards just in the hope of being discovered.

Bonfire night was a big occasion for us and we gathered tyres for weeks in advance. Farmers' silage pits were always a good place from which to steal them. I'm sure if we had asked for them in the first place, we would have probably been given them, but quite often, in the process of taking them, we would trample a field of hay. Looking back now it was hard work but it was all part of the entertainment.

Myself and my mate Neil came up with a plan one day. We made the shape of a large man out of timber. We then got some old clothes and dressed him. We used a cabbage for a head, and once it got dark we took it in turns to carry him down to the main road. We placed him lying on the roadside with his head in next to the ditch with the rest of his body sticking out onto the road. We lay behind the ditch waiting for our first car to come along and we didn't have long to wait. It was hilarious to watch as the driver had to swerve to avoid hitting our buddy. You can imagine his surprise and shock when he got out to see who was lying there. We would lift up our buddy and run up the field and out of sight, but once the coast was clear we set him out again. However, the next car didn't see our buddy in time and drove over his legs. By the time the car screeched to a halt we had picked up our badly injured buddy and once again disappeared out of sight. All the occupants of the car were talking in a foreign language, so we couldn't understand a word they were saying, as they franticly searched for their victim. Later that night we had to run, so we abandoned our buddy, but sometime later, once we knew we were safe, Neil turned to me and said, "I'm just after realising I have lost my Daddy's Wellingtons".

Thank God I never started smoking. I remember my father watching me one day when I was drinking a bottle of mineral. I would have been thirteen or fourteen. At the time, he noticed something unusual about the way I attacked the bottle and said to me, "If you ever start drinking, you will become an alcoholic". How true that would later turn out to be. I was truly blessed that I never saw my parents drunk or abusing alcohol, but I suppose my father was aware that alcohol addiction had been a problem in our family and was worried that I had inherited the addictive gene.

My first memory of taking alcohol was when I was about fourteen. It must have been a special occasion in my father's home as there was a large group of family and guests gathered. When the party was in full swing I sneaked a bottle of drink outside and drank it. I don't know how much I drank or what it was, but I do remember falling and being unable to get up again. The power had gone from my legs. There were five concrete steps leading up to our front door and I had to crawl on my hands and knees to get back inside again.

The following Easter I returned to work in the hotel. This time I was promoted to front hall porter. I was now wearing black shoes, black trousers, a white shirt and black dickey bow. It was almost impossible to keep my shirt clean for a full day. I was always watching over my shoulder, as it was possible to get hit by anything ranging from a dirty brillo pad or dish cloth to a dirty bucket of water. Sometimes I might have the fire hose turned on me and then I would find myself running for cover.

I suppose I gave as good as I got. One day, a waitress broke a raw egg over my head and what a mess it made. It was several days later before I got my chance for revenge. As she was waiting to be served at the hot plate I sneaked up behind her and grabbed an egg and attempted to smash it over her head. What I didn't realise was that the egg had been hard boiled, so as well as almost knocking her out, I nearly broke my hand in the process.

One day we carried a member of staff and placed him on top of an open wheelie bin. This gentleman was very tall and of light build, and his bum got stuck inside the surround to which the black bag was attached. Other staff members had a struggle trying to release him as we had already disappeared.

My hours were now 8am to 7pm, six days per week. Although we spent a lot of time messing about, the job itself could get very busy and sometimes you were under so much pressure you just felt like running away from it all. I had to carry the visitors' luggage and serve tea and sandwiches. I remember that wet days were sure to be busier than dry days as most of the guests would be sitting about and feeling sorry for themselves. You never knew when a bus tour might stop off for afternoon tea and when that happened it was just total chaos preparing and serving their orders.

One day, when I was already run off my feet, I noticed three coach loads stopping outside. They were American tourists. I met them at the front door and informed them that we didn't serve afternoon tea and recommended a nice little café down the street. They had turned to get back on board their buses when the manageress appeared out of nowhere. She approached the busload of tourists and, after discovering what had happened, she said, "Of course we are still serving afternoon tea, so come on in and Martin Jim will take your orders". I would just like to add that I didn't receive any tips for that service.

Another day I was out in the lounge and my job was to take out the ashes and put on the fire. It was a wet day, and as usual a lot of the guests were lying about. I had earlier taken in a large plastic bin full of turf and stored this in the box provided. Although I knew the ashes were hot from the previous fire, I figured I would chance placing them into my plastic bin for transporting outside. It would speed up the whole process as I didn't want to waste time looking for a proper bucket. As I was making my way out through the lounge, I could see and feel the ashes, which contained small pieces of coal, starting to burn. My bin caught fire and I knew I had to start running in order to get it outside the building. The shortest route was through the manager's office, and that's exactly the way I went. The manager and his secretary got a shock as I raced in with my burning bin on my way to the back door of the hotel.

That season I got a pay rise of £3 per week. It was my second season and I was now on £18 per week. One day I found £20 lying outside the manager's office door; I picked it up and placed it in my pocket. I decided I would hold onto it, and wait and see if anyone reported losing it. I figured that if it belonged to some of my mates or another member of staff on similar poor wages, I would happily give it back. After a few days and not having heard anyone saying that they had lost money, I decided to treat myself and my workmate to a day at the funfair that was in town. At work the following day, I still had £10 of my big find left, and I was feeling a little guilty, so I came up with a plan. I went to the upstairs corridor around the time when I knew the manager would be doing his rounds. As he approached, with his usual air of authority, I stopped him and informed him I had just found £5 lying on the stairs. He looked at me and said, "I wish everyone was as honest as you". He thanked me again for my honesty, and continued on his inspection. I went back to the funfair and still had another £5 to spend.

A week later the manager called me into his office, where he told me that since nobody had admitted losing the £5, he was giving it to me. He told me to treat myself to the funfair as I really deserved it.

Another day I was in the dining room preparing sandwiches and a female member of staff grabbed me by my privates. She had caught me unawares and made me jump. I was holding the bread knife in my hand at the time and I accidentally hit her and cut her hand. I felt terrible as she required seven stitches to the wound. Under the circumstances, the details of exactly how the incident happened were kept quiet and not many people knew the true story.

Some nights myself and a few mates would go and play bingo. It was more for the craic than anything else. I would get bored after the first few games and I remember turning the book upside down, thus making it more difficult to mark. I would also let a few numbers get called and try and remember them and mark them sometime later.

Another pastime I enjoyed back then was card playing. There were raffles in different houses and the prizes could vary from a donkey to a goose, or maybe two hens. One winter's evening, we found ourselves playing for a goat. But whoever was lucky, or maybe unlucky enough to win it, would just put it up for raffle again the following week.

Nobody had collected or inquired about their prize in months and when one winner finally went to claim his prize, we discovered that our neighbour James had killed it and eaten it, after he himself had won it at one of the earlier raffles. It later transpired that my brother Edmund actually helped him to butcher it. We had been playing for a long time for a prize that no longer existed.

One night, we were once again playing for the goat. The raffle was taking place in the house of another man who had previously won it. There were quite a few characters gathered around the table, along with the usual serious card players. Someone decided to switch off the lights just as the tea was being served and. on the spur of the moment. I decided to throw a punch at the gentleman seated next to me. The room was in total darkness, but when I heard the sound of my neighbour falling under the table, I knew I had connected. The whole room erupted into a brawl. I jumped up from my chair and was throwing punches wildly in the darkness. When the light was finally switched on, I noticed two brothers were trying to choke each other, and someone had also knocked an old lady to the ground. Since we were on opposite sides of the table, I assumed and prayed silently that it couldn't have been me. The table was also broken, and someone had thrown a pot of jam, which had smashed on the wall.

We found other forms of entertainment at the local youth club. It was held every Saturday night in the parish hall. My mates and I didn't seem to have any interest other than messing about and acting the eejit. One night I got up onto the stage, where there was a large pair of curtains. I grabbed hold of them in Tarzan style, and walking back, still holding the outstretched curtains, I raced out and swung over the open floor. As I was swinging back in again, I could hear the sound of the curtains tearing. I landed on my backside on the stage floor, underneath the now unattached and damaged curtains. When I was confronted about it, I said that I was just imagining myself as Tarzan. The committee eventually barred me and a few of my mates for a period of time. Most of the other lads our own age were trying to court the local girls, but we just referred to them as sissies or mama's boys. Later, after a meeting one night, the committee decided that enough was enough and that was the end of our Saturday night youth club. When our parish priest asked us what we wanted instead, I replied, "A boxing club!"

My third season started with another pay increase of £3. I was now earning £21 per week as a front hall porter. Although I hadn't started drinking yet (I never did smoke), I now had become addicted to slot machines. I remember on a few occasions losing all my wages on pay day. That was a horrible experience. But a few of my mates and I discovered a method of fiddling the machines. First of all, we learned that if you flicked a two pence coin hard enough in the slot it would register as a ten pence piece. Secondly, we discovered that the back panel on the machine could be wedged open enough for us to get our hand inside to hold and control the reels. For a short period of time we were hitting the jackpot every day. Some of the time our winnings would amount to very little as we would just get the two pence coins back again. When we complained about this to the shop owner, we were told that if we hadn't put them in in the first place it wouldn't be happening. Thank God I got away from that habit and never did get into any other forms of gambling.

Some of our mates, by now, owned cars and we soon started playing a very dangerous dare. Two of us at a time would sit on the roof top. Sitting side by side, we held onto each other with one hand, while placing our other hand in the open window. We would hold on for sheer life as the driver raced up the road. It was a miracle none of us ever suffered any serious injuries or lost our lives as a result of that stunt.

But we did figure out a less dangerous form of entertainment – hiding in the boot of the car. After the driver had picked up a passenger, the fellow in the boot would start banging and screaming for help. We found this hilarious and whoever was driving would then turn the music up loud, as if to drown out the cries for help. Whoever was brave enough to go in the boot made sure it was left slightly open, because once you were locked inside you were left there at your mates' mercy. We also discovered it was a great way of gaining free admission to football matches, sports days or stock car racing.

That same season I bought my first motorbike. It was a Honda 70cc. My father gave me the money to pay for it. It cost £300. I was supposed to repay my father on a weekly basis. It was a good job that I hadn't borrowed the money from a bank, because my name would have been blacklisted. Some weeks I gave my father money and some weeks I didn't, but my father never once mentioned it. My parents never took any money from us towards our keep, but I'm sure there were times when they were struggling.

I was all business now with my new motorbike and for the first two weeks I took great care and was very careful on the road. However, as time went on, I became more daring and reckless. One day, myself and my mate Patrick, who had a Honda 125cc, were touring about. We both had passengers. I was struggling all day trying to follow and keep up with him. That evening we were driving down a very steep part of the road with a bridge and sharp corner at the bottom of it. Patrick had more experience as well as more sense, so he started to slow down. I said to myself, "Now this is my chance to pass them and show them how it's done". I didn't ease off the throttle and as I zoomed past I even gave a big wave of my hand just to show off. Johnny, my passenger, was now gripping me harder and harder and needless to say I didn't manage to take the corner. We ended up crashing through the hedge. Luckily we missed the stone bridge. Johnny suffered a broken nose as a result of our tumble. Some time afterwards he said to me, "You know it will be your fault if I never get married." On asking him how he came to that conclusion, he pointed at his crooked nose, saying, "What woman will take me now?"

That was my first accident on my bike, but it wasn't going to be my last. I was so reckless and fearless back then that it got to the stage where anyone who knew me would not sit on the bike with me. I crashed several times with passengers onboard. When I knew they were becoming frightened, it just made me even more daring and reckless, even though I was putting our lives on the line. I would sometimes have sore sides from the laughter.

One night I had two mates with me on my bike. Denis was sitting behind and Seamus was sitting on the handlebars. I was going full throttle down a hill and suffered a blow-out on my front wheel. Needless to say, the three of us got an unexpected tumble.

Another day I was driving home from work and saw Mary, who also worked in the hotel, walking along the road. When I stopped and offered her a lift, she said there was no way she was getting on with me! I promised I would drive easy and after swearing on at least a dozen saints' names, she agreed to accept the lift. Mary was wearing a miniskirt and when she had just about got her leg lifted over the seat, I took off. I didn't give her enough time to place her feet on the foot stands, so as I was now racing down the road, Mary was holding onto me for dear life and screaming her head off. It was only when we reached her house that I realised what had happened. Her bare leg had been touching the bike's hot exhaust pipe. Mary suffered minor burns to her leg, for which I was genuinely sorry.

The following Easter I started my fourth season as a hotel porter. It was also to be my last, as my contract would be terminated abruptly.

The Beginning of the Madness

My wages had now increased to £25 per week. My heart was not in the job anymore. I was approaching my eighteenth birthday and would soon be able to sign on at our local social welfare office and claim unemployment benefit. I knew that amounted to £18 per week so I figured it would be pointless working hard and long hours for £7 extra per week. I also knew I could get plenty of work on the bog with my brother Edmund, which would leave me much better off financially.

After my birthday, which was in May, I informed the manager that I was quitting. When he asked me why, I told him the truth. He then threatened to call the Social Welfare office to say that I had a job, meaning that I wouldn't qualify for unemployment benefit. I wasn't sure if he would carry out his threat so I accepted his offer of a pay rise of £5 per week and returned to work. I knew at that particular time they were under pressure for staff, but I had made up my mind and was determined to leave, one way or another.

I figured out that all I had to do was to get myself sacked and I knew that wouldn't be a problem. As well as not doing my own work I set about disrupting everybody else's, creating mayhem and causing havoc about the place.

A few days later I got my wish and my walking papers. My manager was so annoyed with me that day that he had difficulty in putting a sentence together. I was sure he was going to hit me. My memories of working there are both good and bad. After I got sacked that day, I got on my Honda 70 and arrived up on the bog, where I knew my father and brother Edmund would be working, trying to save our turf. The fact that we had two homes to heat meant we needed to save double the amount of fuel. After I told them what had happened, my father told me not to worry about it as there would be plenty more opportunities. That is one thing I will always be grateful for. Although my father and mother lived in two separate houses, I had the most understanding and loving parents in the world. They were always there for us when we needed them. I always thank God for having them for so long, especially when we needed them most.

That summer I got a lot of work on the bog. Edmund would get the contract for cutting the turf, and he would employ me to do the spreading (known locally as 'in the hole'). The pay was normally £15 per day, so it was lottery money compared to my measly hotel wages.

One morning, Edmund said we had two days work to do for a gentleman who had hired our services. Edmund added that our employer was working in Dublin and that he had paid us in advance, which was a nice gesture. We figured that if we worked really hard we should manage to have the job completed after lunchtime the following day. Well, that's exactly what we did and the following day we were finished in record time, and we stood back admiring our hard work. An acquaintance of ours approached us, and thanked us for doing such a good job. He then informed us that we had just cut his bank of turf by mistake. We were both shocked. Edmund asked someone who was working nearby to confirm who owned the turf we had just cut. Edmund came back, and said "Sorry wee brother, but I could have swore we were on the right bank".

Edmund had met our employer in a pub, and they had consumed a good few drinks. Our boss had taken Edmund up to the bog to show him his bank, and Edmund admitted it was pretty dark at the time. Edmund then suggested to the gentleman whose turf we had wrongly cut to offer us some pay, as it was the least he could do. This same gentleman was a shrewd operator, and he said we would be lucky to cut our losses as he had a good mind of reporting us both to the social welfare for working and claiming benefits. I half expected Edmund then to clock him one, but Edmund turned to me, and said, "We'll get that cowboy later." Although exhausted, we began cutting the proper bank.

On another morning, when we arrived on the bog to work at our own turf, we were confronted by a gentleman who informed us he had a claim to part of our bog. This man had just returned home after living in the USA for a number of years. It wasn't the news we were expecting to hear, and to make matters worse he said that his bank was situated in the middle of what we assumed was our own. He added that he had maps to prove it.

Although we knew it was possible, we went to an elderly neighbour who we trusted would know the truth and tell us accordingly. He confirmed that, indeed, this same character's family had worked there many years ago. Edmund then said, "Well, if that's the case, I will soon put a spanner in his works."

Edmund knew when this gentleman's turf would be ready for taking out and that he would have to use our road. Edmund suggested that we open a new bank along the entire bottom of our bog which would cut right through our road, thus making it impossible to drive on, explaining that this would be the only way to block him.

"Sure, will that not block us as well?" I asked him, and Edmund agreed, but added, "We are still strong enough to carry out the turf, so we will see now how smart he thinks he is."

Edmund and myself got started and spent the first day digging the sod off. We made sure to take off a large amount, thus ensuring the road would be beyond repair. The second day Edmund cut the turf as usual, and as I spread them out, I had to use both sides of the bank to place them on. We had just completed our crazy plan, when the Yank appeared on the scene. He couldn't believe his eyes, and as he looked at our piece of work, he asked, "How the hell do you guys expect me to get my turf out now?"

Edmund looked at him, and said "Did you ever hear of a helicopter?"

The Yank replied, "You guys are bloody crazy; youse have just destroyed the bog."

When our own turf were ready for taking out, we had to fetch a number of long timber planks, and place them across the new road to form a walking bridge for carrying our bags of turf. Although it was a slow and difficult task, we did manage to get our turf home. The Yank never returned to save his turf, and must have decided to give up on the whole idea.

With my earnings from the bog, I managed to buy myself a bigger and more powerful motorbike. It was a Honda 250cc. I bought it in Derry for £180 sterling. It had much more power, but I still hadn't learned any lessons from my previous accidents.

One day, I met my mate John coming from Sunday Mass, on his racing bike. He had a few steep hills to go up on his way home so I suggested I would give him a tow. He was a bit reluctant at first but I assured him I would drive easy. I managed to get my hands on a length of rope and attached it underneath the handlebars of his bicycle, connecting it to the rear suspension of my motorbike.

I started off slow, but kept increasing my speed along the way. I remember looking over my shoulder a few times and seeing John holding on for all he was worth, trying to keep himself and his bike on the road. John admitted that if I hadn't stopped when I did he was just going to let go, as his hands and arms were so tired and weak. It was a miracle that we survived that crazy stunt without injury or worse.

You see, I would just get this buzz inside me at times and very often I put myself and others at risk.

On another day I was out for a spin on my motorbike and was driving past a golf course. I was alone and on the spur of the moment I just drove onto the course and up through the links. There was a large group of golfers enjoying a leisurely round of golf. But when they spotted me, some of them began running in an attempt to get out of my way. A few other players, outraged at my antics, started swinging their golf sticks at me.

As I was racing out of the small exit gate, trying to make my escape, I remember closing my eyes for a few seconds, certain that

The Beginning of the Madness

I would be struck with a club. As usual, I wasn't wearing a helmet.

On another day, I was down in our local village, which was also a seaside resort. There was an amusement arcade which had two rows of gaming machines lined back-to-back up the middle of the floor. The place was packed and every machine was occupied. I figured that if nobody walked out in front of me I would have enough room to do a quick circle of the hall on my motorbike. Once the doorway was clear I raced in, but wasn't prepared for what happened next. As I slowed down to take the corner at the top of the hall, two very angry old women attacked me. One battered me with her umbrella, while the other thumped me with her handbag. The whole place cheered as I struggled to drive out through the mayhem.

One other night, my mate John and I drove into a local nightclub on my motorbike. We drove through the main entrance door into the middle of the packed dance floor. I stopped and revved my bike several times, filling the room with smoke and fumes. The bouncers came towards us armed with batons, and we managed to make our escape out of the exit doors just in time.

There was a track nearby at the Sandy Hills (local nickname for the sand dunes), where motorbike scrambling races were held. I went several times on my 'road bike' to see if I could complete a stage. For the record, I always practised when it was empty. However, as my bike wasn't built for rough ground, I was usually sent flying over the handlebars.

Carrigart Boxing Club was formed in 1980, although a club did exist many years earlier. There was a barn next to the priest's parochial house that was converted into a gym. It was a two-storey building. Upstairs was used for training on the punch bags while downstairs had a boxing ring for us to spar in.

Training was three nights per week, Monday, Wednesday and Friday. It was a great pastime for the young men of the parish, as we now had something to keep us out of trouble. Our trainer had made it clear he would not tolerate any messers in his club. We also went running a few nights a week, so when our first tournament was held in the parish hall, we were fairly fit.

We were both excited and nervous as everyone wanted to impress in front of family and friends at their first big fight. It was a big occasion for all concerned, including our trainers and committee members. On the evening of the fight, I was in the changing room preparing myself. I noticed a boxer from one of the visiting clubs going through his warm-up routine. He had the look and the moves of someone who seemed to know what he was doing, and I remember thinking to myself that I wouldn't like to be the fellow who was fighting him. When it was my turn to box, I climbed into the ring. I was nervous and praying to myself for divine inspiration. Then I heard the compere calling out our names. I knew my opponent was not the fellow I had been supposed to fight and I was horrified when I saw the boxer whom I had been eyeing up earlier, now climbing into the ring opposite me. I turned to my trainer and said, "That's not the fellow I am matched with."

He replied, "Never mind who he is, just go out and box him!"

I did go out and try my best, but I was well and truly beaten and out-boxed in every round. Most of the other boxers from our club won their fights that night, which was a credit to them and our trainer.

We all continued training hard and were well prepared and ready for our next fight. There was a field behind my mother's house that had a very steep incline. Some days before our second tournament was due, I erected a ramp at the foot of it and started riding onto it on an old Raleigh bicycle I had purchased for the sum of £3. I was trying to increase my jump span on each attempt. I remember as I was approaching the ramp my chain came off, thus throwing me off balance. For a few seconds I did consider steering wide of it but must have changed my mind.

My next memory was awakening and realising I was sitting alone in the middle of a field, my head aching and my mind a complete blank. I was frightened and as I rose to my feet I noticed my flying machine lying some yards away. I walked the short distance down to my mother's house.

My uncle Johnny was sitting in his wheelchair at the fire, smoking his woodbine cigarettes, as usual. I asked Johnny what day and what time it was and told him honestly that I couldn't remember a thing. Johnny looked at me and said, "If you don't stop asking stupid questions like that, you will end up in St Conal's Hospital (our local Psychiatric Hospital).

I didn't tell my trainer of my accident as I didn't want to miss the opportunity of taking part. During my second fight, I was hit with a combination of hard punches in the first minute of the first round and ended up knocked out with my arse on the canvass. My opponent launched his attack immediately after the sound of the bell, and caught me unawares. Although my bicycling accident had no connection with my defeat, it was my second time to suffer a knockout inside a week. My boxing career had got off to a very bad start.

On another night, we travelled to a tournament in Kincasslagh in West Donegal. Our trainer insisted we all pay the entrance fee, but my mate Dom and I decided to climb in through a toilet window rather than pay at the door. After a struggle we squeezed through, but then realised we were in the ladies' toilets. Luckily enough, there were no ladies present, so we just put our heads down and walked into a packed hall.

Shortly after that my trainer approached me and informed me I had just been matched to fight. I had to borrow a pair of shorts, and as I didn't have a pair of boxing boots, I just decided to wear the runners I had on my feet. When I climbed into the ring, my trainer looked at my feet, and said, "Are you coming in here to box or pull tug of war?" He was referring to the fact that my runners were big and clumsy, and also the soles were heavy with deep tracks.

I remember my fight that night was tough going. At the end of the second round, I told my trainer that I was seeing six eyes. He said to me, "Well, I suppose you had better aim and try and hit the two in the middle".

After the club closed for the season I never went back, so that was the end of my boxing career. I suppose my boxing record was now pretty similar to my education and employment history – not very impressive, to say the least.

Dom Doherty

My father usually came in to wake me for Mass every Sunday morning. When he sat down on the side of my bed one morning, I somehow sensed there was something wrong. My father had tears in his eyes as he told me that my mate Dom had died in a car accident the previous night. Dom was driving. Dom's two mates, Seamus and Thomas, who were passengers in his car, escaped without injury. There was no other vehicle involved. It was my first experience of the death of a friend, and I was devastated. I could only imagine the sadness and the pain that Dom's family would suffer. Dom would have been a very good boxer, and had the prospects and talent to become a champion boxer. Dom Doherty died 3rd October 1981, aged 18. R.I.P.

Working for the County Council

I got a job with Donegal County Council. It was on a 'Back to Work' Scheme, and although it was only a temporary position it was good while it lasted. We were employed at our local pier, building a slipway for launching small boats and jet skis. The basic pay was £98 per week but, as we had to work according to the tides, it meant there was plenty of overtime and weekend work. There were large wire baskets called Gabriels that we had to fill with stones, tie closed and attach to the next to form a wall that would keep the tide at bay.

There were a few other characters working on this same project, so it wasn't unusual for a scuffle to break out. Quite often some of us would have to find a change of clothes after suffering an unwanted dip in the tide. I was still driving my Honda 250cc, and one morning travelling to work I had yet another lucky escape. The road was covered with snow and ice and as I drove down a hill I skidded and fell off my bike. The bike came to a halt when it hit the ditch, but I now found myself sliding down the road towards an oncoming car. The driver managed to stop just in time. It was a lady driver and she was speechless as she watched me getting back onto my bike. I then gave her a big wave as I continued on my way. Although I was aware of that treacherous icy spot, I still managed to lose control and suffer another tumble in exactly the same place some nights later.

I eventually sold that bike and bought myself another 250cc motorbike. This time I went for a Suzuki, but I still hadn't got used

Working for the County Council

to the idea of paying for tax or insurance. One night, I was driving through my local village and a Garda on duty signalled for me to stop. I thought I would take a chance, so I just kept on going as fast as I could and made my escape.

Shortly afterwards my luck finally ran out when I got stopped at another checkpoint. Later, at court, I was fined a total of £56 for not wearing a helmet, for having no drivers' licence and no tax or insurance.

After the work on the slipway was completed, my Back to Work Scheme came to an end. I was now unemployed again. Although I missed the money, I wasn't too bothered or concerned about going out of my way to look for work. Unlike most of my mates, who were either working, or doing FÁS courses, I was just happy to doss about. I never was career-minded or in any way ambitious. During the summer months, Edmund and I could get plenty of work on the bog; our wages had increased to £20 per day. As I was still in receipt of unemployment benefit I was happy enough with my casual employment. Other times I would get the odd day's work gathering potatoes.

My Nightmare Begins

I remember the night I ordered my first drink at a bar. I was in a local nightclub, and I met an old school mate who was drinking a glass of beer. I had been thinking about trying it again for some time. When I saw Joe walking around, casually holding his prized drink, it was all the encouragement I needed. I went up to the bar, and as I didn't want to make the same mistake I did when I got drunk at home, I ordered myself a half pint of Smithwicks.

I watched Joe to see how often he took a swig from his glass, and I would do the same. After my first drink I was sort of disappointed as it didn't do much for me, so I went back again to the bar, and ordered two more beers, one for myself, and one for Joe. Again I watched and waited for him to take a drink, but from that first night it was obvious that my mate and I had different appetites for the booze. I was getting annoyed waiting for him to finish his drink, and I told him I would rather watch paint dry.

After my second beer I could feel myself feeling a little buzz, so I headed for the bar again. Joe told me he didn't want another drink, but I still ordered two more beers, as I wanted them both for myself. From my very first drink it was obvious that I was going to have a problem with it. If I had the money, I would keep drinking until I was out of my head or sometimes just fell asleep.

During my early years of drinking I got into a lot of trouble in the pubs and the nightclub scene. One night, after a brawl broke out,

My Nightmare Begins

the DJ said he wasn't playing any more heavy metal music as he wrongly assumed that was what caused the fight.

I can't really blame alcohol for all of it, because I was a bit on the wild side back then and got a great buzz from it. Many times, after I came off second best and received a good thumping, I would say to myself, "this craic is no good; I must stop this oul' carry on". But after a few days, when I had started to recover again, I would change my mind and go out looking for a rematch or revenge.

My mates and I were always looking for ways and methods of getting drunk cheap and quick. We tried drinking out of straws and just drinking as fast as we could swallow it. We also bought poitin at £3 per bottle. A few of us also got into the habit of trying to manage a session all day Sunday so quite often we could be found in several different battles before Monday morning.

I had no sense or fear of danger during that time, but there were a few occasions when I had to run for cover because I found myself being attacked with weapons that included bottles, batons and, on one occasion, a chainsaw. I was barred from most bars and clubs in my own and surrounding areas, which meant I often had to travel out of town. Quite often I would end up alone in a bar or a club on the other side of the county. That posed another great risk, because on many occasions I found myself stranded with no transport or money for a taxi fare home. As a result I took shelter in sheds and barns, or just crashed out in a field until daylight.

When my brother Edmund went on a binge, he had a habit of buying a supply of poitin, which he would hide at various locations near his home. Sometimes he would forget where he put them, and more often than not you could find him searching for his precious drink. One time, he placed several bottles in the hedge that ran along the main road at our mother's house. He would try his best to keep it secret from all the family, including me, because he knew that I might decide to treat myself and my mates to some of it.

One evening when he returned home, he was alarmed to find a tractor with a hedge-cutter attached, working at exactly the same spot where he had stored his supply. He rushed over and was devastated to find all his bottles had been smashed. I heard the commotion and rushed out to find Edmund shouting at the driver and threatening to pull him from the tractor.

I asked Edmund "What the hell is going on here?"

Edmund looked at me and said, "That eejit with the hedge-cutter has just destroyed my still."

Another time Edmund and I were moving a stack of turf on our street, and Edmund remarked that we might find a bottle or two in the stack. He had hidden some previously, but never did find them. When we were in having our tea, I sneaked out and filled a bottle with water and placed it inside the stack at the side where Edmund would be working. Once we started back to work, I had to keep my head down as I was giggling and waiting for the big find. It wasn't long until I heard the big "Yahoo", and the next thing I saw was Edmund dancing and singing across the street holding the bottle in his hand. He shouted over to me, "Keep on working brother; I have just struck oil."

I was doubled over with laughter as Edmund opened the bottle and put it to his mouth. After taking his usual large swallow, he quickly realised that it was water. Seeing me in hysterics, he very soon put two and two together. I ran up the field for cover until he settled down and saw the funny side of it all.

On another occasion, I saw Edmund hiding two more bottles, and again I replaced one with water. I waited patiently until I saw him taking a neighbouring man up the field for a drink. I wanted to see the craic, so I casually walked up to them as they were opening one of the bottles. As luck would have it, it wasn't the bottle I had switched, so I had to think of another plan.

My Nightmare Begins

They offered me a drink so I replied, "Oh, I'd better not bother as that stuff puts me clean off my head." Then I added, "Ah, maybe I will," and picked up the bottle that I knew contained the water. I turned to them and said, "Cheers, boys," and finished off the entire contents of the bottle. They both stared at me, flabbergasted.

I then started to put on an act, and after spinning round and round a few times, I ran at my neighbour and wrestled him to the ground. They both shouted at me to settle down, but I continued my act for a few more minutes, dancing and shadow boxing around them, and challenging them both to fight. They were both relieved later when I told them the truth.

Another day, Edmund and I heard a car crashing just a short distance from our mother's house. When we arrived at the scene of the accident, we found the car overturned on its side, and for some reason the driver had disappeared. We got a strong smell coming from the car boot, and could see some spillage. At first we thought it was petrol, but when we got the boot door open we discovered a barrel inside, which was now half full of poitin. We were delighted and from our excitement, you would think that we had just won the lotto.

We realised that the driver had been on his rounds, supplying various public houses, before his mishap, so needless to say we took the barrel home with us. We didn't feel bad about taking it as we figured it would save us having to buy it later from a crooked publican. It was a peculiar incident because it occurred on a 'Good Friday'. I suppose the publicans and the driver picked that particular date because all public houses should be closed, and it would be an ideal time for doing their dodgy deal.

On another occasion, the local Guards arrived at our mother's home. The Sergeant informed me he had a warrant to search our house, as he believed we might have some poitin. His suspicions were well-founded. I knew that Edmund had several bottles in his room and was, at that very moment, in there having a drink, and wouldn't take too kindly if he had to part with his carry-out.

The Guards had made it as far as our kitchen when Edmund suddenly appeared from his room. The Sergeant, who was leading the posse, was holding a clipboard with the search warrant attached. When he informed Edmund about the reason for his visit, Edmund stared at him, and said "Is that so?"

I wasn't surprised when Edmund gave the Sergeant a thump with his fist, knocking him to the floor. Although I had no sympathy for the Sergeant, I didn't want Edmund in any more trouble, so I tried to hold him back, before he could launch an attack on the other Guards. The Sergeant, who was recovering from his blow, had picked himself up from the floor. He pointed his finger at Edmund, saying, "We will get you for this."

His threat made my blood boil, and I suggested that he should get out of our house quickly, before I set Edmund loose. They did retreat and we later discovered the search warrant and clipboard lying underneath our couch. Edmund was charged with assault, and narrowly avoided going to prison.

On other occasions, we would buy the kit and make our own brew of beer. We would add extra yeast and sugar to make it stronger. We also purchased a large plastic rubbish bin, complete with its lid and used this as our container, thus ensuring we could make larger brews. Usually it would just taste horrible, but we didn't care as it was only the effect we wanted.

I remember one time when I was on a wild binge of poitin and home brew. My brother Eunan arrived to give me a lift to our local Garda Station, where it was compulsory to sign on every week for your dole or unemployment benefit. When he looked at me and saw the shape I was in, he asked, "Do you know what day of the week it is?" I replied, "Yes, it must be Tuesday, but what month is it?"

After returning from a nightclub one night, I brought my mate Pat in for a drink of poitin. I had decided to make punch out of it.

My Nightmare Begins

So, after boiling the kettle, I produced my bottle and made what I assumed to be two good strong drinks. It was some time later that I discovered that I had been serving us both Doon Well holy water!

One day, I was gathering potatoes for a local farmer and found a bottle of poitin in the field. I didn't know or care how old it was and after drinking it I climbed out over the fence and went in search of more drink. That night I ended up in a nightclub, still wearing my work clothes. I also got into another one of my battles and received a wound on my arm that required ten stitches.

On another occasion, a group of us were fighting outside a different nightclub. I went there knowing there was going to be trouble. I had been drinking all day and had consumed a large amount of alcohol. During the scuffle, I went crashing through a large glass window. I was only wearing a t-shirt and received another large cut to my arm that required thirty-six stitches – eighteen stitches internally and eighteen externally. My two mates, John and James, and I were then arrested and put into the same patrol car. On our way to the hospital, I grabbed the Garda's hat and placed it on my own head.

Once inside the hospital, I hopped into a wheelchair and raced down a corridor almost knocking the Garda over in the process. He was so disgusted with me that he remarked, "You're not near right in the head, racing about there and the arm hanging from you". He then stormed out, and left us there.

Another mate, Paddy, who had also been involved in the fight, then arrived at the hospital to check up on me. Paddy had brought his girlfriend along for company, and while they were waiting for me to get stitched up, they sneaked into the next cubicle and started getting very passionate. It wasn't long until a nurse heard the moans and groans of the love birds, and I could only laugh as I watched her wallop Paddy with a towel, and chase them out the door. Paddy and his sweetheart did wait for me, and gave me a very welcome lift back home.

Some nights later Paddy called at my house, and I was very amused to discover he was wearing a doctor's coat which had a stethoscope hanging from its pocket. As the nurse was chasing Paddy and his girlfriend from the casualty department, he somehow managed to steal the coat from the doctor who was sewing my arm back together. We all got summoned to court for that night's events but it didn't really bother me at the time, and thankfully our penalties weren't too severe.

My Accident

At weekends, I used a local bus service that would take us to and from a nightclub in a town about twenty miles away. There were live bands playing and it was always busy, so it was the place to be for the craic.

As usual, I was there one Saturday night and met Anne, who was home on holidays from Glasgow. Anne was very attractive, and had a great personality. I also liked her Glaswegian accent and her witty sense of humour. We hit it off from the beginning and arranged a date for the following night, in the same venue.

I didn't go drinking during the day on the Sunday as I wanted to be sober, so that I would impress Anne. I was really excited and looking forward to my date. At about nine o'clock I went down to my local village where I got the bus. The bus was always packed and sometimes you had more craic travelling on it than in the actual nightclub.

I met Anne as arranged and we had a really nice time. We talked, we joked, and we danced. Anne was staying at her aunt's house, and I travelled home with her on her bus. Anne was returning home to Glasgow the following morning. We exchanged contact details and promised we would see each other again. Then I set off walking for home, which was a distance of about seven miles.

It was the 25th of August 1986 and I was aged twenty-three. Although I was tired, I was really happy and looking forward to talking to and hopefully seeing Anne sometime in the near future. In spite of having consumed quite a large amount of drink, I was still fairly steady on my feet. I would run for short distances, then resumed walking when I got tired. The last thing I remember is approaching a part of the road that had a bad corner with a dip in the road.

My next memory is waking up with my family by my bedside. I was in the Intensive Care Unit in Letterkenny General Hospital. I was told I had been struck by a car at about 5am and, due to the circumstances – it was still fairly dark and I was wearing dark clothes – the car driver was in no way negligent or guilty of careless driving.

I had suffered horrific injuries to my body. Both my legs were shattered. My knees and ankles were badly broken and my shoulder, hip, pelvis and groin were also injured. I was in so much pain that I cried for mercy. When my father asked the doctor the chances of my survival, the doctor just shook his head and said it didn't look good. My only hope was transfer to a Dublin hospital. As time wasn't on my side, they said they would have to transfer me by helicopter.

Although I didn't know it at the time, as we were waiting for the helicopter to arrive, my brother-in-law Daniel Cannon, a patient in the medical ward of Letterkenny General Hospital, lost his long battle with cancer and passed away. Daniel was married to my sister Mary Teresa, and they had two sons and two daughters. Daniel was a gentleman and true friend. In fact, I had confided to him the previous week that I had been summoned to court for a variety of offences, including assault and malicious damage (another bar room brawl).

None of us knew then how ill Daniel actually was. Shortly before Daniel passed away, he asked a family member to look into the case I was due to answer. I hadn't made anyone else aware of my bagful of summonses, because I didn't want my family worrying, and I was assuming I could keep it secret unless I received a prison sentence.

A storm started blowing, and the helicopter coming to transfer me to Dublin had to be cancelled, and a much larger and heavier

My Accident

helicopter was sent for. As I was being transferred from ICU into the helicopter, Daniel Cannon's funeral arrangements were being made. We both left the hospital at the same time on our different journeys. I can only imagine how difficult it must have been for my family.

Daniel Cannon died on the 26th of August 1986, aged 49. R.I.P

I do remember travelling in the helicopter, even though I was drifting in and out of consciousness. The nurse who was travelling with us held my hand, which was comforting.

I was admitted to the ICU ward of Dr. Stevens' Hospital. My family remained at my bedside for the first two weeks, since my chances of survival remained at only 50-50.

One day, when the nurse was dressing my wounds, I saw for the first time the extent of my injuries. My groin, thighs, knees and ankles were just a mess of blood and bones, and it was horrific to look at. I was really shocked and my first thought was that I could never recover from such serious injuries. I went into a sort of a panic attack and started asking the nurse all sorts of questions, hoping for some sort of reassurance. When my doctor told me that my leg might have to be amputated I was devastated. As I lay in my bed trying to come to terms with my predicament I almost gave up my will to live, because I felt that I didn't have the energy or the stamina to battle for recovery.

Having my family at my bedside and knowing how much they loved me and wanted me to recover was what gave me the inspiration to fight against the odds. My parents would recite the Rosary as they sat by my bedside, and we would also pray to St Anthony, asking for his help.

My mate Martin told me that he was at home when he first heard about my accident, and that he went into his bathroom, locked the door and cried his eyes out. Before he came out, he prayed one Our Father and ten Hail Mary's for me. I thought that was very thoughtful of him.

I received Mass cards from friends and neighbours on a daily basis, and I have since read that a single Mass offered for oneself during life may be worth more than a thousand celebrated for you after death.

It wasn't easy for my family to visit me on such a regular basis, but they were always by my side. From our home to Dr. Stevens Hospital was a good five hour drive each way, so it must have been very difficult for them to arrange transport. Sometimes they would travel by car and sometimes by bus. The driver of the car involved in our accident also visited me on a regular basis, which I appreciated. I reassured him that he should not feel one bit guilty or bad about our accident as it was in no way his fault.

After two weeks in the I.C.U. I was transferred to a large eighteen-bed ward. Although I was out of immediate danger, my recovery was going to be slow and painful. It's funny how you tend to take your health and wellbeing for granted, and it's only when it's taken away from you that you realise it. I was totally dependent on the excellent care of the nurses, and they sure were a dedicated and caring group.

At first I was slightly embarrassed as they applied dressings to my groin area and also when they would assist me in my toiletry needs, but as time passed I got used to it all. My injuries required extensive surgery. I had plates and wires inserted in both my knees and ankles. I also had to have extensive skin grafting to large parts of my body, mainly my groin area and both my legs.

My friends and neighbours visited me on a regular basis. One of them brought me a Walkman radio cassette player, which gave me endless pleasure. Even today, when I hear the songs from that period it reminds me of my time in the hospital: 'Thorn in My Side' by The Eurhythmics and 'You Can Call Me Al' by Paul Simon are two that come to my mind now. The young nurses would be singing along as they went about their work.

My Accident

My friend Anne came over from Glasgow to visit, and spent some days at my bedside. That was really special to me. It gave me a strong desire to walk again as Anne said she would love to have me spend Christmas with her in Glasgow. As I was very conscious of the injuries and disfigurement to my groin and legs, it was a huge boost to my morale and self-esteem to know that Anne wanted to see me again. As I watched Anne walk out of my ward for her return trip to Glasgow, I knew I was falling in love with her, and I couldn't wait to see her again. Receiving and writing love letters to Anne during that period gave me great comfort and something to look forward to.

One day, my brother Edmund walked into my ward. I was delighted to see him. He was well dressed and steady on his feet, but somehow I knew he had been drinking. He was on his own, or so I thought. When he sat down at my bedside and said, "That was some handling," I hadn't a clue what he was talking about, and I was almost afraid to ask. He then went on to explain that our neighbour James had wanted to come with him to visit me, and as Edmund was now alone, I asked, "Did he change his mind?"

Edmund said, "No he didn't, and that's the funny thing about it." (James was the character who was involved with Edmund when they both butchered the goat). Edmund then told me that he and James had been drinking all through the previous night, before going to Milford village to get the 8am bus to Dublin. They were early for the bus, so they decided they would try to buy a bottle of whiskey to drink on the journey down to Dublin.

Edmund started knocking very hard on one of the doors of a pub in the village, and when the publican/landlord finally opened the door to see who was there, a misunderstanding took place between himself and Edmund. Both of them thought the other was going to attack, so then the two of them began wrestling and falling in the pub door. James tried his best to get them separated and settled at the same time as he was watching out for their bus.

Amid all the mayhem and confusion, Edmund and James managed to explain their case, and when the publican realised it was only a bottle of whiskey they wanted to purchase, he was only too happy to oblige. After giving them the bottle he also gave them a few doubles each on the house. "We were both in great form as we boarded the bus," said Edmund.

James didn't have any money, and after paying for the bottle Edmund only had just enough for the two return tickets, which he put in his pocket. Every so often, as Edmund was telling me the story, he would go silent and hold his head in his hands. I would encourage him to continue as the curiosity was killing me. Eventually I heard what happened.

At some stage of the journey they both fell asleep, and as the bus was approaching the traffic lights on the outskirts of Dublin city centre, James awoke. The lights were now red and the bus had stopped. Not realising or caring where he was, James made his way up the bus to the exit door. As he walked out of the bus, he shouted back to the startled bus driver, "I'm away to the toilet as I'm bursting for a slash". The lights changed and as the bus was moving off again, the driver looked back, and saw James waving his arms in the air as he staggered across the busy lanes of traffic.

When the bus reached the depot, the driver woke Edmund and explained what had happened. Edmund was worried, as he had the return bus tickets, and his mate was now lost somewhere in Dublin, with not a penny in his pocket. James had never been in a city before; in fact, it was his first time out of his own neighbourhood. We both hoped that the Guards might have picked him up before he came to any harm.

After visiting time was over, Edmund left the hospital and managed to get the return bus home to Donegal – alone. That night, I didn't sleep much as I was worried for our friend. I also felt sort of responsible as they wouldn't have been coming to Dublin had they not wanted to visit me.

I was both surprised and delighted the following morning when James walked into my ward with a woman on his arm. What we didn't know was that James had been writing to a pen pal for some time. He had made contact with her through the *Ireland's Own* magazine. The lady in question was from the north side of Dublin, and somehow James had managed to make his way to her house. I asked him afterwards how he got there, but he told me he hadn't a clue. He said the last thing he could remember was getting on the bus in Milford – a village about 13 miles from our home place. James spent a few days in Dublin with his friend before returning home.

I remember the day I was told of Daniel Cannon's death. Even though it was some weeks later, the doctors had advised my family that I was still too ill to receive such sad news. The visitor who broke the news to me probably was unaware that I didn't know, as he apologised immediately and seemed genuinely embarrassed.

I broke down crying and a nurse came over to comfort me. She told me I had enough to worry about to ensure my own recovery. She suggested we both say a prayer to Daniel, which we did.

I asked her if she could take me to a phone as I wanted to ring my sister, Mary. Both my legs were fitted with plaster, one full cast and one below my knee. The kind nurse then got me into a wheelchair. She placed a large board underneath my behind and my leg to support the weight of my full cast.

The payphone on my floor was out of order so the nurse then brought me down in the lift to the floor below. Although I still couldn't walk, it was a great feeling to get a break from my ward and be in new surroundings. The nurse said she would leave me to talk in private and would come back for me in ten minutes.

I had finished my call before the nurse arrived back, so I decided I would try and make my own way back to my ward. I managed to wheel myself over to the lift, and I figured that, if I reversed my chair into the lift, I would be able to drive straight out at my own floor.

I got into the lift without a problem, but once the doors closed I realised I was in a bother. My leg with the full cast was now protruding about two feet out from my seat, which prevented me from getting in close enough to press the lift buttons. I found myself stuck inside a lift that was stationary. I'm not sure how long I was there, but it seemed like ages. After a lot of effort, I managed to slide far enough out of the chair to reach the button, but by the time I was seated again, the door had closed again. I tried that same stunt, with exactly the same results, on three more occasions before my nurse in shining armour came to my rescue.

The thirst I had in the hospital was unreal. One day it was so bad that I chewed the drip that was going into my vein. I had been watching the liquid flowing through the tube and couldn't resist it. The hospital was also located beside Guinness Brewery, and I could smell the aroma of the fresh Guinness on a daily basis. I craved a drink, and I used to imagine myself lifting and swallowing a pint. When I started to recover and was allowed to drink minerals, I always made sure I had a good supply beside my bed. I suppose it was part of my addiction and related to my alcoholism. One day, I asked the lady who was going around the wards with her mobile shop for a few bottles of mineral. She had nine bottles in her shop. She counted thirteen stored in my locker and underneath my bed.

I had now been in hospital for three months. The plaster casts had been removed from both my legs and my wounds were healed, but my skin grafting was very tender to touch. The physiotherapists were working with me on a daily basis, but as soon as I put any weight on my legs,, I would feel faint and so weak that I would have to sit down before I collapsed. The physiotherapists persisted in their exercise plan and increased their visits to twice daily but getting me back on my feet unaided again seemed to be an impossible task. One day the kind physiotherapist had to dry the tears from my eyes as I found the whole experience overwhelming. I didn't have the energy to continue and became overcome with emotion as I imagined myself being confined to a wheelchair on a permanent basis.

One morning at about 3am, I awoke with a strong feeling that I could walk again; I had a strong desire to get out of bed and put my instinct to the test. There was another patient also awake in the bed next to mine. He had the power of his legs, so I asked him to get me a walking frame. I got myself out of my bed unaided, and taking hold of my walking aid I took my first steps. It was an unbelievable experience and I was so overwhelmed that I let out a loud "Yahoo!"

I knew from that moment that I was on the road to recovery and could walk again. I did, however, get reprimanded by the night nurse for getting out of bed unattended, and waking the other patients with my antics. Once I was given the gift of power in my legs again I didn't hold back, and I kept walking and walking around the ward and surrounding area. I could feel myself getting stronger each time.

A few days later I was taken to theatre. As my left knee had been completely shattered, with most of my knee cap missing, I could not bend my leg. In theatre they froze it and tried to force some movement or flexibility. After applying pressure without any success they had to stop, otherwise it would have just broken. My doctor then told me there was not much more they could do for me, so I could start making arrangements for going home to Donegal.

I was told I would never regain full movement of my right ankle and that my left leg would remain permanently straight. The first thought I had then was that I wouldn't be able to kneel at Mass.

Even though my injuries were horrific, I do have fond memories of Dr. Stevens Hospital. The love and the care that the staff offered me will always be close to my heart. I remember endless occasions when I was in pain or feeling sorry for myself, that the nurses sat by my bedside, holding my hand and comforting me.

As I got on the hospital bus outside Dr. Stevens hospital, I was dressed in my pyjamas, bedroom slippers and dressing gown. I didn't have any clothes, as they had to be cut from me when I was first admitted to hospital on the morning of my accident. Not only that, I had lost almost three stone in weight during my stay in the hospital.

It was the end of November. The frost was thick on the ground and I was really cold. My family had offered to come down by car and give me a lift, but I reckoned I would be okay on the bus. I suppose it was my rough and ready attitude, but I was also thinking of saving them the hassle. I was so happy and so excited. When we stopped at a café in Co Monaghan on our way home, I couldn't go in so the bus driver kindly brought me out a cup of warm tea and a sandwich. I really enjoyed and appreciated it.

My family met me at Letterkenny General Hospital with a new outfit. It was a great feeling that night, getting dressed in my new clothes and going home with my family. Although I had made a miraculous recovery, I still had a long way to go. I was still dependent on the aid of two crutches and was told I would require extensive physiotherapy three times weekly for an indefinite period of time.

I met with the social welfare officer and learned that I had three months' disability benefit to collect and cash. I had more money than ever, so I decided I would treat myself to a well-deserved drink. Although I had been previously barred from all the local watering holes, I decided I would chance my luck. The first publican assured me I was welcome and served me my drink. My mind was working overtime and somehow I didn't feel he was genuine. I assumed he

My Accident

knew I had a wad of money in my possession and that I wouldn't pose any threat due to my circumstances.

After a few drinks I told him my interpretation of the situation, so needless to say he re-imposed the ban. The next public house I entered was pretty much the same. I was served my drink and still wasn't happy, so after a man-to-man talk with the landlord, he also reinstated the previous ban. As all these pubs were located close to each other, I'm pretty sure they were sharing notes as I hobbled and limped about on my crutches on my soon-to-be-curtailed pub crawl.

As I entered the third pub, I wasn't sure what kind of a reception I was going to receive. Regardless of getting served or not, I was sort of revved up and wanted confrontation. I suppose I wanted to let the town know I was still alive and not to be taken for granted. Although I was served several drinks, it wasn't long until a battle broke out and, needless to say, I got arrested for assault and criminal damage using my crutches as my weapon.

The Garda patrol car took me back to my mother's house and as I was getting out of the car, a neighbour was on her way in to visit. When she heard what I had done, she said to my mother, "Sadie, I know what must have happened to him. When he lost all his blood in the accident, it was replaced with a madman's".

My mother replied "Sure he was mad from day one".

I was also charged for that offence. but the court was lenient enough on me. I do think the judge had sympathy for me because I had miraculously survived my accident. The previous charges before my accident had been struck out while I was recovering in ICU. I suppose they assumed I had enough on my plate at that particular time.

After being involved in such a serious accident and now getting a second chance at life, I still hadn't learned my lesson or copped on to myself. I was wild before my accident and maybe I was now just trying to prove a point to myself. Although I was still dependent on my crutches, I was very unpredictable once I entered a pub, so in a short time after my return from hospital I found myself barred again from most of the bars with which I had a history. It must also have been a trend back then with the publican/landlord association to send out letters from their solicitors informing me not to visit them. The postman seemed amused as he had the added hassle of delivering them, and on several occasions I received letters from public houses I hadn't even been in warning me in advance not to visit.

My first appointment at the physiotherapy department of Letterkenny General Hospital got off to a very bad start. I found the exercises painful and difficult, and I was also suffering from a hangover. I got talking to another patient, who was a bit of a character, so we decided to go for a drink. My companion was also on crutches.

The physiotherapists had shown us our exercises and had left us alone to do them while they attended to the other patients. We just left without bothering to make another appointment, and walked, or should I say hobbled, down the street and into a bar. We both got very drunk. I never saw that gentleman, whose name I forgot, after that day and often wondered how he got on.

That night I got a taxi home. The driver stopped outside our gate. As I was walking up towards our gate, I forgot about the cattle grid that had been fitted in my absence, so my left crutch went straight down in between the bars. As I was trying to balance myself, I stuck the second crutch between two more bars. So, left without any support, I then fell flat on my face on the ground. I had to crawl up the driveway, but eventually managed to make it up to our door.

Even though I never did return for any further physiotherapy, I found myself walking without my crutches. I was becoming fitter and stronger on my feet day-by-day. I walked every day, and was always trying to push myself that little bit harder each time.

My First Time Out of Ireland

Anne and I were in regular contact by letters and phone. I was looking forward so much to seeing her again. I made arrangements to go to Glasgow so that we could spend Christmas and New Year together. I got a bus in Carrigart, which took me to Glasgow for £46 return. The ticket would remain valid for three months.

It was a big occasion for me, as it was my first time out of my own country. As we travelled into Glasgow, I must have fallen asleep on the bus, because I remember awakening as we were going under a flyover bridge. I almost had a heart attack when I saw a large lorry driving across it. I thought the bloody thing was flying in mid-air!

As we arrived into Glasgow, I was nervous and excited and so relieved when I saw Anne rushing to greet me at the bus terminal. We had a really nice, peaceful and happy Christmas together, and I suppose we were only really getting to know each other.

When Anne said, "When we do have our fall outs, we will have so much fun making up again," I thought to myself, "what would we be falling out about, sure we are so happy together." I suppose that showed how naive I really was.

Anne brought me to visit her family, where I received a warm welcome. Anne's friend invited us to her house for New Year's Eve, and that was when our fairy tale romance hit its first trial. As the party progressed, another guest started winding me up. Anne had asked him to stop several times, without success, so I hit him a thump which sent him tumbling onto the top of a large leafed table, which was already laden down with drink. It collapsed under the weight of my sparring partner. I was asked to leave by the house owner and I was pleased when Anne accompanied me out the door.

It was early morning New Year's day and as we were walking down a street I noticed a lot of cars parked outside a building. My head was so far gone. I suggested to Anne we go in for a drink, until she informed me it was actually a church and Mass was going on. I hadn't a clue what time of day or night it was and thought we were outside a packed nightclub.

When we finally got back to Anne's flat, she said we needed to have a serious talk about my drinking and my behaviour at the party. When Anne said she believed I had a drink problem, I just didn't want to know. I did know I wanted more drink that morning and rather than stay and face the music, I went off on my own against Anne's wishes. She pleaded with me to stay and talk things over, but I suppose I was too hot-headed and selfish to listen.

I found myself drinking alone in various bars in and around Glasgow city centre that day, and ended up in another fight. I never was interested in football and didn't realise Celtic and Rangers had been playing earlier that day. To make matters worse, I was wearing a big green jumper that Anne had bought me for Christmas.

As I was trying to make my way back to Anne's flat, I asked a gentleman at a bus stop for directions. He said, "Clear off, Paddy, and get out of my sight."

I asked him what was his problem, and he replied, "I'm a Rangers supporter, and I'm in a foul mood today as we got beat by you Papish so-and-sos." Not knowing who or what I was dealing with, I lashed out and hit him a thump, but when I tried to follow it up, I missed him and hit the side of the bus stop with my fist. My opponent then raced off up the street swearing loudly that he would be back to sort me out.

A lady who was also waiting for the bus advised me to get off the streets immediately. When I told her the address I was going to, she suggested I get a taxi, and that was when I realised I didn't have any money left. The lady then hailed me a taxi, and she was so kind she also paid the fare required.

When I got back to Anne's flat, Anne said she was worried sick about me. Anne was anxious for us to talk, but as I was totally wrecked I just fell asleep on the sofa. We did spend the next few days talking and making up, and Anne said she was prepared to give me another chance.

After the New Year, Anne returned to her office job, and I returned home to Carrigart. We continued writing love letters, and I would go to our local village every Saturday evening to call her from the public phone box. There was a phone in my mother's house, but I wouldn't want to make the habit of using it, as you could easily lose track of time.

One particular evening, as I was talking to my sweetheart, a local character drove up in his car and parked outside the phone box. He wanted to use the phone, so he started blowing his car horn, thus making it impossible for me to hear. I had to end my call much sooner than normal and I wasn't very happy.

I walked on past the car as I wanted to give the driver the impression that I wasn't going to bother about him. But when he entered the phone box, I sneaked back and discovered he had left the car keys in the ignition. I got into his car, and drove it tight against the door of the phone box. He was well and truly trapped, while I started shadow boxing outside and making funny faces at him. For good measure I hid his car keys, and my sides were sore from laughter as I made my way back home.

I managed to remain sober and out of trouble on my next two trips to Glasgow, and Anne and myself both declared our love for each other. We really missed each other when we were apart, so we decided we would get engaged with a view to getting married. We also agreed I would move to Glasgow on a permanent basis as Anne had her own home, and a secure job.

Since we didn't have any date planned, we decided we would try to spend as much time together as possible in the meantime. Anne suggested that I should re-sit my exams or do a training course, both of which were sensible options. I didn't want the commitment that this would involve, and I was happy to just doss about leading my carefree lifestyle. I was expecting to receive compensation from my accident at some time in the future, and I was under the impression that once that was sorted everything else would fall into place. Looking for a job never crossed my mind.

Anne picked the engagement ring herself in Glasgow, and came over to Donegal for the weekend to celebrate with my family. She helped me to pay for the ring, as I was only in receipt of disability benefit.

We all went out for a meal and a drink on the Friday night and had a really nice time. On the Saturday night, however, I got involved in a punch-up in a local bar. I was trying to calm an argument between friends and lost my temper when I was also asked to leave. I remember throwing punches at the landlord and anyone else who tried to have me removed from the premises.

During the melee the shirt I was wearing was ripped off. It happened to be one that Anne had just bought for me, and she threatened to call off our engagement. It took me sometime to get her to settle down and to agree to give me another chance. Anne returned home to Glasgow and we continued keeping in touch by phone and letters.

I was still attending Dr. Stevens Hospital as an out-patient on a regular basis, and it was also possible to get called in front of an insurance board at short notice. As my parents never took any money from us for our keep, I suppose I didn't have any financial worries. I just tried to save enough money for my next trip to see Anne in Glasgow.

My brother Edmund was also living in Glasgow at that time, so I used to look forward to meeting up with him. Anne really liked

Edmund and she was happy for us to catch up, as long as we didn't go off on a binge.

One day when Anne had gone to work, Edmund called out to visit me and when he asked, "Do you fancy a pint wee brother?" I answered, "I would love a pint but I don't have any money." Edmund assured me he would soon take care of that problem. He suggested that he would take me around a few of his haunts, so I soon found myself on a pub crawl in the Barras and Glasgow Cross area.

Edmund seemed to know so many people and, although I was watching the clock in the beginning, I lost track of time. Even though I knew I should be returning to Anne and spending my time with her, I just couldn't seem to walk away from the drink and the craic.

That night I went home with Edmund and crashed out at his place. The following morning when I awoke, I could only laugh as I listened to Edmund singing happily as he went about preparing our breakfast. I knew I would have some explaining to do to Anne, but deep down I wanted drink that morning more than anything else. When Edmund placed a large fry in front of me, he said, "Remember when you told me yesterday that you didn't have any money? Well brother, we are now both in the same boat, as I'm skint also."

We were both craving a drink so Edmund came up with a plan. He took me down to his Social Security office and I approached the lady on the counter and told her a big sad story. I explained that I had arrived in Glasgow three days previously with no money and no place to stay. I told her I had been sleeping in an old car and hadn't eaten in ages. She took pity on me and directed me to another office, where I would receive counter payment. She told us what bus to get, but as we didn't have the fare we started off walking.

That same day, Edmund and I somehow ended up walking onto the middle of a motorway, holding on to the crash barrier to keep from falling out in front of the traffic. I can't remember how on earth we got onto it, but we had to walk for ages to reach an exit. I still wasn't that steady on my feet and I remember that every time a large truck would pass, we would have to hold tight and hope for the best. We eventually managed to get off it.

Later, at traffic lights, I was making an attempt to cross the street, when Edmund shouted for me to wait, but I replied that it was okay as "the wee green man is on". When Edmund again hesitated, I asked, "are you waiting on any particular shade of green?"

Edmund replied, "Don't rely too much on that wee green so-and-so as he might let us down." Eventually we reached our destination and I received a payment of £29. I felt rich, because when you're skint and desperate, £29 is a lot of money.

We went into a nearby pub for a well-deserved drink, where I ordered double whiskeys so fast that Edmund said to me, "Remember, it was only £29 you received and not £290, you wee head case".

That night, I made my way back to Anne's flat, but I was drunk and totally wrecked. I remember leaning against the door as I rang the bell. When she opened the door, I fell in flat on my face and collapsed on the hall floor.

Some hours later I awoke and I was frozen. As I stumbled down the hallway, I peeped into Anne's bedroom and I could see she was asleep. I made my way into the spare room, knowing I had messed up big time as I tried to remember the previous day's events.

Anne told me that, although she loved me, she couldn't put up with my drinking or wild living any longer. She said she was calling off our engagement, and asked me not to call or write to her since she wouldn't be changing her mind. Even though I was expecting it, I was devastated and all broken up, but I knew I had only myself to blame.

Before I walked out the door Anne gave me a hug, and said she genuinely hoped everything would work out for me in the future. I wished Anne likewise and said I wanted her to know I would always love her. The tears were running down my face as I got the bus for my return journey home. It seemed like my world had been torn apart. Anne was a beautiful girl, and I knew she would have a queue of men looking to win her affections. That thought alone added to my pain, even though I genuinely wished Anne success and happiness in the future.

Back at home I really missed Anne and wondered how she was getting on. Although I was tempted several times to call her, I didn't, because I was hoping that she might have a change of heart and contact me.

My Life of Mayhem Continues

I continued going off on drinking sessions and behaving recklessly and getting myself into dangerous situations. My family were very concerned and worried about my behaviour, but I refused to take their sound advice and was unaware of how dangerous and dark a journey I was on.

One night, after yet another fight, I ended up damaging my knee. I had to go back into Dr. Stevens' Hospital for another operation, because the pins and wires that had been holding my leg together were now protruding out through my skin graft. As I waited to be taken to theatre, I was told that my operation was cancelled as an emergency had cropped up. By now I had made friends with a girl from Co Galway, whose operation was also cancelled. The exact same thing happened to both of us on two more occasions.

On the fourth day, we still were waiting and fasting from midnight. It was 4.45 pm and we were both starving. We assumed our operations were going to be cancelled once again, so Claire fetched a large cake somebody had brought her. After I had devoured my half, the porter from theatre arrived to take me for my operation. I was now in a bit of a predicament. I didn't want to have to cancel again, so I said I was still fasting.

As I was coming out of my operation, I imagined my head was stuck to the table and I couldn't move it. For the short space of time it lasted, I remember feeling frightened. I don't know if it was the side effects of having eaten the cake, or if anybody else ever had a similar experience.

My Life of Mayhem Continues

After my operation I was transferred to a three-bed ward. One of the patients in the ward with me had crashed his motorbike, while the other was a big man who had come second in a fight. Both were confined to bed. The biker now had a good supply of beer by his bedside, presents from his biker friends, so we were rich with cans of Smithwicks. On the second night after my operation, my biker friend asked if I would like to have a drink with him. I gladly accepted.

I was acting the role of barman and asked if I should give our boxing friend a drink. The biker replied, "No way. He might get out of bed and half kill the two of us."

We both got drunk that night in our ward. I remember a nice young nurse saying to me, "It's up to yourself what you do with your life. If you want to destroy it, then that's your own choice."

When I was getting discharged, my doctor told me I would most certainly develop arthritis in both my legs, but mainly in my left knee and right ankle. He also advised me to go back for physiotherapy on a regular basis. Needless to say, I never did and continued on drinking and living life on the edge.

I went into a bar one night and was really annoyed when I was informed that I was barred. I honestly hadn't done anything; in fact, I had actually stopped my mates from wrecking the joint on a previous visit. I went in behind the bar counter to confront the manager, but he ran away, thus leaving me in charge of a bar full of drink. On that particular night, the bar was very busy as there was a karaoke final taking place. I wanted a drink, so I decided to serve myself, and felt sort of important for a short time as I took full control of managing the place. Needless to say, I served a good few customers free drink, and I didn't have any hesitation in imposing barring orders on some of the hob knobs of the parish that were present.

I don't know how long I had been behind the counter when I noticed the patrol car screeching to a halt outside the window. The guards rushed in the door in a line and I remember counting five of them in total. The whole bar fell silent and I suppose the guards were a bit confused for a few seconds, as they probably expected to come into a small riot.

The sergeant who was leading the raid looked in at me as I was silently going about my new job, so I says, "Sergeant, I'm sure glad to see you," and I pointed to the bar manager and said, "I want him removed immediately from my premises."

As there were so many guards, they didn't have any room to place me into the patrol car so, after cautioning me, they advised me to go away. I then cheekily asked the Sergeant to drive me to another pub I wasn't barred in. He told me if I didn't disappear he would arrest me and take me to the station, so I told him that if he had to pay for his petrol he wouldn't be so fond of driving and joyriding about. I went on to add that it was me and other taxpayers who were paying for his petrol. That really annoyed him, and he clenched his big fist and says, "You've never done an honest day's work in your life." I suppose the two of us were sort of right in our assumptions about each other.

Later, at court, I received a one month suspended prison sentence for assault and causing criminal damage. I was also ordered to keep the peace and observe good behaviour for a period of three years. In fairness to the guards and the publican, they didn't charge me for larceny. Even though I wouldn't class myself as a thief, helping myself that night to free beer and several bags of peanuts could have easily warranted such a charge.

My solicitor wrote me a sharp letter stating that he was not very impressed with my behaviour. He advised me to settle down and keep on the right side of the law. He warned that another court appearance would result in me being sent to prison, which would seriously damage and affect my claim for compensation.

I was now really missing Anne, and as I was more than likely to get myself into more trouble at home, I decided I would go to London and try to make a new life for myself until my compensation case was settled. I remember when I told my father about my plan he looked at me, and said, "You know I'm going to miss you, but please God the change will do you good." Daddy then gave me a small bottle of holy water, and made me promise I would continue going to Mass on a Sunday, and not to forget to say my prayers on a daily basis.

Going to London

I had an appointment in Dublin coming up at the end of August with doctors from the insurance board, so I made arrangements to get the boat later that same night for my onward journey to London.

While I was waiting for my bus to take me to Dublin, a gentleman whom I didn't know approached and asked me for some money. I offered him whatever loose change I had in my pocket. He didn't seem very grateful and said, "Can you not do any better than that?" I knew now I had made a mistake in becoming involved with him. I didn't want to give him any paper money and I knew from his manner that he wasn't just going to forget about it and walk away. He was also much bigger than me and as he became more aggressive I told him to calm down and I would see what money I had in my pocket.

I now had butterflies in my stomach, because I knew I had to box him one. I took my chances and hit him a right hook, hoping to catch him off his guard and get myself out of town in one piece.

That same evening, as my bus was leaving the depot, I could see a posse out looking for me, and I was very relieved to make my escape. I didn't fancy going into my medical check-up in Dublin with two black eyes or worse.

I managed to make it to Dublin in time for my appointment, and was so relieved when my check-up was over. I was feeling both excited and nervous, thinking about my move to the big smoke. I had over four hours to wait until I got my bus from Dublin city centre to Dun Laoghaire Port, where I would get the boat to Holyhead in North Wales. From there I would get another coach to Victoria Coach Station in London. It was an overnight sailing and we were due to arrive in London about 7am the following morning.

I had £250 sterling in my possession so I decided I might as well spend whatever remaining punts I had left. I started on a pub crawl and after drinking a few pints of lager, I started knocking back double brandies. I can remember being very drunk on the boat but I don't recall either embarking or disembarking. The next morning, I remember waking up on the coach on the way to London and being seated next to a nun. God knows what bullshit I was talking while I was awake. The kind nun gave me a beautiful pair of Rosary beads and said she would pray for me.

We arrived on time Wednesday morning at Victoria Coach Station, which is located in the heart of London. My mate Frank was there waiting for me. Frank lived in Acton, west London and had told me I could stay at his place until I got myself sorted. Frank had travelled by tube (underground train system). This form of transport was going to be a whole new experience of travelling for me.

As Frank ushered me through the vast throng of passengers pushing and rushing about their journeys, I must admit that I found it a somewhat daunting and mind-boggling experience. I wondered how I would get familiar with all the different networks and for a part of that journey I began to wonder whether I had made the right decision in moving to London.

It was still early morning when I arrived at my new digs. After being shown my room, Johnny, another one of the lodgers – whom I knew and hadn't seen for quite some time – appeared and after giving me a big bear hug and welcoming me to London, suggested we go for a drink.

Although I had planned on going to bed for a few hours and then checking out my new surroundings, I found Johnny's offer to hard to refuse. We walked the short distance to a pub to which Johnny said he liked to go occasionally for a quiet pint and which he felt would be an ideal place for us to have a good catch-up. Needless to say it ended up in another all-day session.

The next morning Frank woke me at 6am and gave me a lift down to Shepherds Bush, also in west London. There was a contractors' office there where I could look for a job. I knew one of the managers personally and Leo told me that if I was ever in London and wanted a job, to give him a shout.

After welcoming me at the office, Leo then sent me with a foreman called Mick out to a job which was close to London-Liverpool Street tube station, in north-east London. We travelled by tube, and I was once again amazed as the passengers hustled and bustled, almost knocking each other down as they scurried to either get off or get on at their intended stops.

Since I was only a labourer, Mick put me to work sweeping and just tidying up around the yard. It was a beautiful sunny morning and I noticed several other workers had removed their shirts, so I was happy to follow suit as I loved the sun and having a nice tan always made me feel good. At lunchtime Mick asked if I wanted to go for a pint and I gladly accepted as I was really thirsty after my previous day's drinking and also from the scorching heat. After four pints we returned to the job with both of us in good form.

It felt great to be back working again and I was now looking forward to my whole new life in London. It was nearing the end of the shift and Mick asked if I was interested in some overtime, which I accepted. Then, shortly after 7pm, Mick said we would go for another pint and that he would put me in for four hours' overtime. We headed back to the same bar that we had been in earlier and after consuming another four pints, we made our way to the tube station.

Mick suggested I should stay at his place that night and we could travel together in the morning out to the job. It sounded like a good idea at the time. Mick was living in Shepherds Bush. Once we sat down on the tube, Mick fell asleep, so at every stop I had to shake him to ask him where we were. When we finally arrived at Shepherds Bush tube station Mick suggested that we go for one more pint before we went home.

As usual, one led to two, and two to three and so on. A number of pints later Mick turned nasty towards me. Mick was born and bred in London and we were drinking in his local. It seemed to me that with him being my boss and me just off the boat, he probably thought I'd listen and take it. So when I told him that I thought he was full of shit, he asked me if I knew where I was and who I was talking to. When I replied that I didn't give a damn he apologised, we shook hands, and ordered another drink.

While we were staggering back to his house, he explained that his wife would probably rear up on us in the beginning, but for me to keep quiet and just ignore her, as she would eventually calm down. True enough, once we entered the house, we were met by one very angry woman. But once she was finished shouting her head off at Mick, she then turned her anger at me and ordered me to get out of her home. I thought to myself, "My first day isn't going so well now." As usual, my wild streak took over and I told them to stick their house where the sun didn't shine and that they were both welcome to each other.

After leaving their house I found myself walking down a strange street in London, drunk and not knowing how far I was from my digs. After walking for what seemed like ages, I flagged down a taxi and gave him my address. I can't remember how much it cost, but when I finally did make it back to my digs, my roommate Noel was getting up for his work. It was only then that I realised the time.

I turned and made my way down to East Acton tube station, feeling the worse for wear from the lack of sleep and the amount of alcohol I had consumed over the past few days, but I suppose I was still excited about my move to London and was still on a bit of a high. After I figured out which platform to go to, I waited for the train that would take me out to my job, where I would face the music again.

I arrived at the site on good time and just continued what I was doing the day before, which was very little, mostly walking about with a yard brush in my hand. It was nearly lunchtime when Mick arrived and I knew from the way he looked at me that he wasn't too pleased to see me. When he asked a few of the other lads beside me to go for a pint, and ignored me, I knew my days in my new job were numbered. But I needed a drink myself, so I headed off on my own to the first pub I saw.

After a few pints I went back to the job as I still wasn't in the form for eating. After Mick and I exchanged another few funny looks at each other, he finally approached and said, "That was some aggro last night". I nodded in agreement. He then asked if I remembered much about it. I said I remembered everything about it and I wouldn't forget his wife ordering me out of their house in the middle of the night.

He replied, "If you think that's bad, she put me out as well and I ended up sleeping in the shed!" That probably explained his shabby appearance and I couldn't help but laugh at the whole experience.

I went to work on Saturday and Sunday and nobody seemed to bother or care what I was doing. Although I would have been saying a few short prayers daily to St Anthony for his protection, I did drift away from my obligation to attend Mass. I didn't bother going to work on Monday, because I was going to have a look at a room in a house in North Acton that I was interested in renting.

Frank told me I would be elected if I got in there as it was a great house for parties. After meeting with the three girls who were already living in the house, I took the room and moved my stuff into what was to become my new digs. Needless to say, my stuff was easily moved since I didn't have much luggage.

A previous occupant of the house had left a sleeping bag behind, so I opened it up and just used it as a duvet cover. Two other lads also moved into the house, so there were now six of us sharing. The house itself was a large, three-storey building, the ground floor of which was occupied by a twenty-four hour mini cab service.

My brother Edmund had arrived back in London, and was staying out in Hanwell which was also in west London. Edmund had lived in north London for a period some years earlier. On Tuesday morning, I travelled back down to the office in Shepherds Bush to meet Edmund; Leo had also promised him a job. I had intended on going on out to my own job, but Mick, my foreman, was also there at the office and when he saw me, he told me that I was sacked for taking Monday off without asking him.

Part of me was mad, but I also felt relieved, because I knew it was only a matter of time before something else went wrong. Although Leo was willing to send me to another job, I decided I needed a few days off as I wanted to register with a doctor, to see if I would qualify for disability benefit and maybe get my rent paid as well.

I managed to get an appointment with a doctor whose surgery was a few doors down from my digs. I had letters with me from my own doctor in Ireland, detailing the extent of my injuries. After examining me, my doctor suggested that I would be much better off staying in Ireland and that he couldn't understand what brought me to London in the first place. I explained that I needed a change since I was about to crack up and that I also thought I might get better physiotherapy. Eventually, he gave me a cert declaring me unfit for work for one month.

After that, I made my way down to my local DHSS office and made my claim. The girl who was interviewing me was more than understanding and, after hearing about my almost fatal car accident, said I would qualify for a counter payment. That was what I had been hoping, because as well as receiving some money, which I badly needed, it also meant that my claim was granted and I would receive my payments on a fortnightly basis.

My landlord had given me a letter stating how much rent I was paying, so the next morning I travelled the short distance to Ealing, west London, where the Housing Benefit Department offices were based and made my claim for rent allowance.

I felt good now that I had all that business sorted out and I noticed that I was getting much stronger and fitter on my feet, due to all the walking and rushing to catch tubes and buses. I was also getting more familiar with the underground.

I went back down to the office on Thursday, as I had four days' wages to collect. I was sent out to another job close to London-Liverpool Street tube station. That suited me fine as I could get the Central Line direct from North Acton tube station, which was within walking distance to my lodgings.

Things were looking good once again. This time I was labouring to a concrete gang. The work was heavy, but after I got over the first week, I became more and more able for it. After I collected my first full week's wages, I decided I would check out the Windmill pub on Acton High Street, as I had been told that was where all the lads from home drank and it was the place for the craic.

As I was enjoying my drink and soaking up the atmosphere, the landlady approached me and asked if my name was Martin Jim. I said it was. She told me that she heard I was very wild back at home and was wondering if that was true.

I asked her name and she said, "You can call me Amy".

I then replied, "Yes, Amy, it's true. I was wild back at home and guess what? I'm still very wild."

Amy said she didn't care what people said about me as she thought she was going to like me. Later that night, in the Windmill pub, I got talking to three girls. When I told them where I was living, they said they had heard it was a great house for parties and that I should let them know when the next one was taking place. I asked them to explain exactly what they thought a good party was, as I was only new in town. They said, "One where you just listen to some music, have a drink and maybe a dance and whatever."

So I suggested that we should have one of those parties right away, because I was anxious to find out what 'whatever' might turn out to be. At closing time, we formed a kitty and bought a big carry-out of drink. Back at my house, we got the music blaring and started dancing on tables, chairs and just going crazy around the house. It wasn't too long until we had everybody else in the house awake. Somehow I did manage to make it in to work the following morning.

A few months later I was still in the same job, but I was also beginning to hit the bottle much more. We were going to the pub at lunchtime and most evenings after work as well. It wasn't long before I started missing shifts and turning up in the mornings really hung over.

One Friday morning, instead of going to work, I decided I would go out to Luton and meet up with a few mates who were living there. The night before, I had borrowed £50 from my work mate, Pat, so I thought I had better square up my debt first.

I arrived out on the job about 10am wearing my best clothes and was met by Drew, our foreman, who asked me if I knew what time it was. I told him I had no intention of starting work and only came out as I wanted to see Pat. Drew asked me to stay to dump a load of concrete, which had already started to go hard. He said if I did that, I could then go and he would put me in for the full shift. Pat also asked me to stay and offered to give me a helping hand. I stayed, but a few hours later, soaking in my own sweat, I was on the train to Luton.

I managed to make it out to the job on Monday morning, but I was feeling wrecked after my weekend drinking, so I didn't stay for the full shift. Needless to say, that night ended up in another big session. Tuesday and Wednesday were pretty much the same.

When I opened my wages on Thursday, I noticed that I had been docked, so I felt really annoyed with Drew about it, even though I was in the wrong and knew I was messing him about.

I had heard from another mate who had worked on a site nearby that there was a pub near us that played good music and had strippers performing during the day. At lunchtime, I suggested to Pat and another lad called Enda that we should go there for a pint. As the three of us approached the bar we were met by the first stripper. She was holding a pint tumbler, half full of pound coins, so we soon added three more. We were just beginning to enjoy our pints when we were approached by the second stripper who, after teasing us with her assets, relieved us of another three pounds. There were three strippers working, and at the pace they were approaching us, I knew it couldn't last much longer.

Enda suggested a few times that we just should leave. It was only six weeks to Christmas and he didn't want to lose his job. I didn't know what was going through Pat's mind, but I was delighted when he ordered three more pints. Once again, we were approached by one of our lady friends, but this time I just put a ten pence coin into her collection. She was furious with me and demanded, "Do you not think I'm worth more than that?" I said she probably was and threw a two pence coin into her glass. For a second I thought she was going to hit me with the tumbler, but after shaking her head in disgust she moved onto Enda, who was unaware of what had just occurred and coincidentally threw in another ten pence coin. After staring into the tumbler in disbelief for a few seconds, she then started yelling at us and called over the bouncers to have us removed. As we were being escorted out, Enda pointed towards the tumbler in the stripper's hand and asked, "What miser put the penny in?"

On the way back to work, myself and Pat were laughing at the craic, but Enda seemed anxious about his job. Once we arrived on site, Enda said he was going to speak with Drew, as he wanted to know if he could finish work a little bit earlier in order to go into the office in Shepherds Bush to sort out a mistake in his wages. When he explained this, Drew said it wouldn't be a problem, but to Enda's dismay, Drew then told him not to bother coming back as he was sacked.

On hearing this and seeing the expression on Enda's face, I just burst into laughter. Drew then turned to me and asked what I thought was so funny, since I was also sacked, and we should take Pat with us on our way out. That certainly wiped the smile from my face and as Enda walked off the job I followed in silence. Neither of us looked for Pat to give him the bad news and once we got outside the site gates we both went our separate ways. That was the last time I saw or heard of Enda and Pat.

The fact that I had qualified for both disability benefit and rent allowance was a huge bonus to my circumstances and it meant I didn't have to worry about holding down a permanent job. One of the girls I was sharing the house with advised me to save enough money for the fare home, because, as she said, "You never know when that might be". It was good advice, but somehow I never managed it.

When I first moved into my digs, I noticed there were two housing benefit cheques coming in the post for a gentleman and a lady whom I knew didn't live there. They had either been living there before I moved in, or else they didn't exist at all. What I did know, however, was that whoever was lucky enough to get the post, could cash them for themselves. As I was the biggest dosser in the house, I got most of them. I used to take them to a publican in east London who would charge £5 for cashing them.

It was a good arrangement while it lasted. One day, after I had cashed one, I continued drinking until closing time. I left the pub and waited for the last bus to Acton, only then realising I didn't keep the price of the fare home. I now found myself stranded, and knew I had to get off the streets, because I knew at least two other men who had been mugged around the same area. Even though I didn't have any money to lose, I certainly didn't want to get beaten up, so I figured that if I could find a safe place to lie down for the night, I would then walk home in the morning when it was clear.

As I was walking about looking for my nest, I noticed a large flat roof at the rear of a public house. I figured this would be a safe place as I would be up off the ground and out of sight. There was a wall about four feet high going around the perimeter of it, so after climbing onto it, I managed to get up onto the roof. There was a TV aerial at the corner, so after hanging my white shirt on it, I moved into the centre and lay down. I must have fallen into a sound sleep soon after that, because it was bright and clear when I awoke the following morning. It was a strange experience waking up that morning on a rooftop, and one that I would not like to experience again. After putting my shirt back on, I had great difficulty getting back down on the ground as I was suffering from the shakes. Thankfully, I managed it eventually without suffering any injuries.

Although I hadn't planned on going home for Christmas, I changed my mind when Frank suggested I should travel with him in his car. I didn't have much money, but it didn't matter, as I knew that once I got home I would be okay. That was the beauty of being at home. You always had a nice warm bed, food in the fridge, and if you had any beer money that was an added bonus.

When my father asked had I far to travel to find a church, I didn't want to confess that I didn't know, so I lied and told him it was only a ten minutes' walk. Looking back now, it hurts me when I think of how much worry I caused my parents with my alcoholism.

One time, my father placed two burgers on my dinner plate, and I noticed he didn't have one himself. When I offered to share, my father said he was okay, and it would do him more good watching me eat it. He often said to me that he wished I would meet a good woman and settle down as he wouldn't be around forever. My father was over fifty when I was born. He was a smart man and he knew that time was not on his side. I never wanted to hurt or worry my parents, but as long as I continued drinking, I was going to be in trouble and getting myself into all sorts of crazy situations.

Back in London, I continued living life on the edge. I used to tell people that my digs at Horn Lane were similar to a train station. There were always different people coming and going and it was the house for anybody and everybody to have a party in. I sure did get to meet some great characters there, both male and female.

One Monday morning, I got a phone call from my solicitor, telling me I had to be in Dublin for 11am the following day for an appointment and a medical check-up with the insurance company. It wasn't the news I had wanted to hear because, as well as being really hung over, I had never flown before and had never seen the inside of an airport. There were still quite a few party revellers present in the house and when I came off the phone I broke my bad news to them. They had no hesitation in forming a kitty which amounted to £180 and I was lucky to also have my money from my benefit cheques.

After a quick shower, I threw a few things into my bag and headed for Heathrow airport. I approached a girl at an Aer Lingus desk and explained my situation. I was nervous and craving for a drink. When I told her that I had never flown before, she had the nerve to ask me how I got to London in the first place. I replied by asking her, did she ever hear of a thing called a boat? Eventually, after all the confusion, I purchased a return ticket to Dublin. I decided I would get the last flight out of Dublin the following day, as that would give me plenty of time after my check-up.

After I got my luggage checked in, I made my way to the bar and ordered a double brandy with a dash of port. After knocking that straight back, I then had three more, so for now, I was well cured. My nerves had settled and I was now looking forward to the rest of my journey. I also got talking to another couple who were getting the same flight as me, so I just sort of followed them and assumed they knew what they were doing.

On the short flight to Dublin I managed to consume a few more quick brandies. I was in top form as I booked myself into a B&B in Dublin city centre. After eating what was to be my only meal that day, I went on a pub crawl around Dublin city centre. That night I ended up in a nightclub on Harcourt Street, called Copper Face Jacks.

The next morning I awoke with another serious hangover and, after a quick shower and a very light breakfast, I decided I would walk to the Mater Private Hospital for my appointment. I was hoping the walk in the fresh air might clear my head a bit. Although I was craving a drink, I decided I would suffer until after my appointment.

When the doctor finally called me into his office, he told me to get undressed and hop up on the couch and he would have a look at me. I found the doctor's attitude very abrupt. I took my time as I wanted to try and convince the doctor that the extent of my injuries were still having serious implications for me (thus assuming this would result in an increase in my compensation claim).

After struggling with my clothes and complaining about the pain and discomfort, I finally got up on his couch. After a quick examination, the doctor told me I was a very lucky man. I asked him how he figured that one out. He said, with the extent of my injuries I was lucky to be so well, I snapped back at him by saying he was the lucky one as it didn't happen to him. After another struggle getting dressed I left, and hobbled down the street out of sight and into the first pub I came to. After getting the cure, I spent the rest of the day in Dublin going from pub to pub, before making my way back out to the airport to get my flight back to London.

I had met and got to know Pete, another great character, whom I enjoyed going drinking with. One day, as I was making my way to Pete's flat, I was approached by a gentleman who was standing outside a barber's shop. This same gentleman informed me he had just opened for business and was awaiting his first customer. He suggested I should take the opportunity of availing of a nice trendy haircut and invited me in. At that particular moment a haircut was the last thing on my mind but after some more persuasion I agreed and a short time later I was seated with the barber working passionately at cutting and styling my hair.

As I looked around I noticed the price list, which I thought was quite expensive and then it suddenly dawned on me that this would leave me with less money for the drink that I was so desperately craving. So I informed my hair stylist that I wasn't in a position to pay his requested charge and suddenly I noticed the change in his expression. He stated clearly he needed full payment, but I began arguing my case and told him I didn't request a haircut and he had in fact invited me in. The barber had now stopped working and as I looked in the mirror I knew I needed him to finish what he had started as my hair was now a complete mess. After some more arguing and bargaining he reluctantly agreed to accept half of what his asking price was and started back cutting and shaping my hair.

Prior to this we had been happily chatting away but now there was silence. When he had finished I had a brief glimpse at myself in the mirror and after handing over the reduced fee I made my way outside and continued towards Pete's flat. As I was sharing my experience with Pete, he burst into laughter as he informed me that my hair stylist had in fact left me with a complete bald patch in the back of my head. The barber had got the last laugh.

As I was coming to terms with my predicament, Pete then informed me he had good news for both of us as he had just received a cheque from social security and he would treat us both to a good drink.

Later that same day, as we were in high spirits, Pete suggested we should head to Soho, the famous red light district in London's West End. Looking at me, Pete added, "Sure the experience will do you good 'Jim.'"

As we travelled by taxi I was thinking to myself if only my parents seen me now. It was bad enough to be missing Mass, but now I was on my way looking for a prostitute with a big bald patch in my head.

The taxi driver dropped us off at a particular club and as we entered we could hear soft music playing in the background, I got an eerie feeling about the whole set-up. A giant of a man approached us and asked what we were looking for. When Pete told him we wanted some nice female company, he invited us to follow him upstairs to meet with some girls who "would give us a good time".

At the top of the stairs, we were introduced to a lady who was sitting behind a desk filing her nails. She told us what was on offer and what each service cost but explained that all the girls were busy at the moment, and asked would we like a cup of tea while we were waiting. I asked if I could use the toilet, and said I would love a cup of tea. I wasn't too long in the toilet, when I heard the commotion and a row breaking out.

Pete had gone behind the desk and after pouring two cups of tea he went looking for me. Pete walked into the first room he came upon, and when he discovered an orgy was taking place, he asked, "Would any of youse fancy a cup of tea"?

When I got out of the bathroom I was also asked to leave, and the bouncer followed behind as I made my way down the stairs. Outside the door, I found Pete lying on the ground complaining of a sore knee. He asked me how I got on. I told him that I didn't get on at all. The police arrived, but when I said we were leaving as soon as we got a taxi they seemed to be happy enough with that.

Getting a taxi proved to be very difficult as the black taxis would not go outside of the square mile radius. Eventually, I managed to hail down a mini cab that brought us back to Acton.

Pete and myself continued on our drinking binge and every day Pete was complaining about his sore knee. On Saturday evening, we were at a house party when I decided I should phone for an ambulance for Pete, who seemed to be in severe pain.

After phoning for the ambulance I then rang for a mini cab for myself as I thought I would head down to a pub in Acton. My taxi arrived before the ambulance and, needless to say, Pete hobbled out and into the taxi with me. When we arrived at the pub the landlord refused to serve us. So, while Pete waited outside the door, I went across the street to a phone box and rang for another ambulance.

I told Pete to stay where he was, as the ambulance was on its way. I said goodbye and good luck and then headed off, walking up the street towards another pub where I figured I would get served. I hadn't gone too far when I heard Pete swearing and shouting at me to wait for him. I turned back and put my arm around him and between staggering and swearing and laughing, we fell into another pub.

This time we did get served as it was a bar that all the hard drinkers and characters drank in. After a few more rounds of drink and listening to Pete complaining about his sore knee, I rang for the third time and ordered another ambulance. The good news was that we did wait for this ambulance. We were happy enough as long as we were getting served, but the bad news was that Pete's knee had been broken all that time. I heard later that the police called at the house where I rang for the first ambulance, so I was probably very lucky I wasn't arrested for wasting their time and making hoax calls. I did genuinely want an ambulance every time I rang, but we just didn't have the patience or sobriety to wait for it. Pete was admitted to hospital for a period of time, where he had a plaster fitted to his leg and eventually made a full recovery.

I got started on several good job opportunities, but due to my alcoholism and reckless character, they all ended prematurely. Leo sent me out to a job in the famous Kew Gardens, in south-west London. Kew Gardens comprises of 300 acres of gardens and botanical glasshouses. The director of the Royal Botanic Gardens, Kew, is responsible for the world's largest collection of living plants and the gardens attract more than 1.35 million visitors per year. My employment at Kew ended abruptly when I crashed the cherry picker machine that I was driving into a large greenhouse and smashed several large panes of glass as a result.

On another occasion, Leo sent me to a job in Rotherhithe in south-east London, unaware that I had been previously sacked from this same job. I hadn't asked Leo to which site I was going and it was only when I got out of the work van that I realised our mistake. As I was admiring the progress that had taken place since my last visit, the foreman appeared and had the pleasure of sacking me twice from the same job.

Amy also got me started on a job with the brewery and my duties were to help load the truck each morning before setting off around the various bars and clubs in London, helping the driver to make his deliveries. As much as I loved that job, I lost it when I failed to show up for several days.

I received another call from my solicitor. This time they wanted me home for three more appointments with doctors, acting on behalf of the insurance company. The first appointment was for Monday morning in my own local Letterkenny General hospital and the other two were in Dublin on the following day.

On Sunday morning, I packed my bag once again, but figured I could afford a few drinks and the fare home, so my first stop was the Windmill pub. I wasn't very long in the Windmill when I knew I had dipped into my ticket money so, instead of facing up to my predicament I headed next door to the Blarney Stone, where I knew a live band would be playing. I continued on drinking there until around 10pm before getting a taxi to the Galtymore nightclub in Cricklewood, North-West London.

Going to London

It was one of those days when you can drink yourself sober again, and after the band had stopped playing, I went up to the food bar for a chicken and chip supper. After paying for my food, I had five pounds left. A girl then came up and stood beside me and after placing her order we got talking. She told me her name was Leanne; she was from London and living in Ealing.

When I asked her for her full address, she asked me why I wanted it. I told her I was after finishing a wild binge on the drink and knew I wasn't going to be able to sleep for the next couple of days or nights so, if I had her address, I would write her nice love letters to help me pass my time. She looked at me for a moment or two, then she just burst out laughing and asked the girl serving us for a pen and a piece of paper.

After writing down her details, Leanne handed the piece of paper to me. It was a serviette. At this stage I had just finished eating my meal and, after wiping my face with her addressed serviette, I then threw it over the counter. I apologised and after receiving another addressed serviette, I did exactly the same thing. This time Leanne just walked away leaving me standing alone at the counter. I was sure now I had blown my chances.

Once outside, I noticed a bicycle sitting alongside a railing so I thought I would borrow it to take me back to my digs. However, what I failed to notice was the chain and padlock attached to it. As I attempted to mount the bicycle I then felt a tap on my shoulder. I was certain it was the police, or whoever owned the bicycle, and was so relieved when I discovered it was my friend Leanne, who asked me if I would like to come back to her house in Ealing for a drink.

Things were looking bright once again, at least for the time being. I decided I would try and forget about my appointments in Ireland and would worry about them at a later date. Back in the house we were joined by Leanne's friend and her date and I insisted on buying some drink as I didn't like coming to a party empty handed. Leanne then walked up the street with me to an all-night cafe, where I managed to purchase four cans of lager at one pound each.

When we returned, I explained to the other couple that I was after making a huge decision – should I buy four cans and keep the bus fare home to Acton in the morning or five cans and walk it? Leanne's friend told me that her fellow and Leanne would both be going to work in the morning, so she suggested we would go for a drink after that, which also sounded like a good idea at the time.

I didn't get any sleep at all that night. I remember looking out the window as morning broke and beginning to panic with reality sinking in. Here I was in Ealing, on Monday morning, with a one pound coin to my name, when I should have been in Letterkenny for the first of my appointments.

I shouted goodbye and good luck as I headed out the door in a hurry, without explaining the predicament I had gotten myself into. In my panic, I forgot to ask Leanne for her phone number, and I never took a note of her address. I decided I would also walk the whole way back to Acton and by that stage the rest of my housemates would be at work. It meant I wouldn't have to talk to them and could just go to bed and get some sleep, as I was completely wrecked.

When I finally arrived at my house, my mate Joe was still there. He laughed when he saw the state I was in. He said, "I thought you went home yesterday", and I said, "Don't ask, it's a long story". Joe then asked if I had any money. I knew what he meant but I said, "Sure, I can give you a pound if you're stuck".

We both laughed at that. Joe would have known I was broke. After getting a sub from Joe for £250, I threw some cold water over my face, changed my shirt and headed, once again, for Heathrow airport. This time I had no bag to pack, as it was still lying in the Windmill pub from the day before. I figured out that even though I had missed my first appointment, all going well, I would still manage to make it to the other two the following day in Dublin.

My Horrors on a Jet Plane

After arriving at Heathrow airport and buying a return ticket to Dublin, I went straight to the bar as I needed a couple of drinks to calm my nerves. I was beginning to go into the horrors and was feeling very paranoid. My shirt was all creased as it hadn't been ironed. I ordered a triple brandy with a dash of port. My hands were shaking badly as I tried to raise the glass to my mouth. I held the glass with both hands and made my way towards the corner of the bar where it was quiet. There I managed to get it swallowed in one go. After ordering the same again and getting it into me, I could feel a hot flush hitting me and I started to relax. I was talking and praying to myself and promising St Anthony that if he got me through this siege safe and well, I would give up the drink.

I was seated next to a woman on the plane and during the flight I started going into the horrors once again, hearing voices in my head, which I imagined were of men who were plotting to attack me and cause me serious injury. I also imagined hearing them saying they would follow me and wait until I was on my own before launching their attack. By now I was frightened and felt so alone. I was wishing I had someone with me, as I knew I had a bad journey in front of me.

One of the air hostesses must have noticed my state of panic, because she approached me and asked if I was okay. My mind was racing, and as I wanted as much help and sympathy as I could get, I told her I was after getting very bad news from home – both my parents had been out on a boat and had got lost at sea. After sympathising with me, she then asked if she could get me anything. I said I would love a large brandy.

Holding the glass with both my hands again, I tried to raise it to my mouth, but this time I was shaking so bad I couldn't hold it and spilled it over the lady next to me. She called the air hostess over again and asked to get moved to a different seat, which made me feel twice as paranoid. I did try to apologise but she just ignored me and, as she got out of her seat, she wiped my precious brandy from her clothes. As far as that lady was concerned, I was on my way home to a terrible tragedy and she didn't even have the manners to offer me her sympathy.

After getting off the plane, I made my way into Dublin city centre. I had now decided I would get a bus back home to Donegal and travel down again in the morning, as it would be a lot safer for me than spending the night in Dublin. I knew I wouldn't be able to relax in Dublin without drinking, and that thought alone added to my anxiety. I was also hoping that once I got seated on the bus, I would get some badly needed sleep. There was still another two hours to wait until my bus would leave, so I knew I couldn't sit in the one place for too long.

I started walking around Dublin city centre in a sort of a circle. Passing a shoe shop, I decided I would buy myself a pair of runners, as I was wearing a big pair of heavy black shoes. I wanted something cheap and light so, after making my purchase, I continued on my way wearing what I thought were my new runners. Walking as hard as I could, I thought I noticed people staring at my feet but at first I just put it down to paranoia. It was only after some time, when my feet started to burn, that I looked down and realised I was walking around Dublin in a pair of bedroom slippers. It was luck that I still had my shoes with me in a carrier bag so, after quickly changing back into them I threw my bedroom slippers over the bridge and into the Liffey River.

I made my way to get my bus and en route I decided to buy a bottle of mouthwash as I was conscious of the really heavy smell coming from my breath. I spilled some and swallowed the rest of the mouthwash before I hopped on my bus for Donegal. I sat at the rear, hoping I would doze off.

When I noticed two men walking towards me, I once again imagined hearing them talking to each other, plotting their assault. I imagined them to be men whom I must have had a previous battle with and that they were now coming for revenge. When they took their seats in front of me, I rushed up to the driver and asked him to put them off the bus as my life was in real danger. The driver told me to get back into my seat as I was annoying him and everybody else on the bus. It seemd to me that the driver was also part of the plan and my paranoia and fear increased.

I then sat towards the front of the bus, next to two old ladies and began telling them about my accident. I was talking fairly loud as I wanted everyone to hear my sad story and was secretly hoping that somebody would have sympathy for me and save me.

When we stopped in Co Monaghan for a fifteen-minute break, I kept close to the two women. I knew they couldn't save me, but at least I would have witnesses who could inform my family and let them know what hospital I was taken to, or whatever.

For the remainder of our two and a half hour journey from Co Monaghan to Letterkenny, I moved seats several more times as I was now afraid to fall asleep. As the bus was pulling into the depot in Letterkenny, I was standing at the front and once the doors opened I made a run for it up the street as fast as I could go. I was looking over my shoulder every so often, to see if I was being followed.

As I reached a café, I decided I would be safer in it, so I ran in the door and scrambled over the counter. One of the girls who was working there must have sensed that I was suffering from the horrors. She kept talking to me and telling me that I was safe and, after getting me a seat, she gave me a cup of tea. The Gardaí arrived on the scene before I had time to either drink it or spill it and after placing me in the back seat of the patrol car they brought me to the Garda station. It was probably the first time I was glad to get arrested, as I felt safe. I don't know how long I was there before I became overcome with fear once again.

When the Guard phoned my brother Eunan, I grabbed the phone from his hand and told Eunan to bring a gun with him as my life was in danger. When Eunan arrived at the station, the Guards were happy enough to release me into his care and we made our way home to Carrigart.

My father was waiting anxiously for me and had a meal prepared, which I wasn't able to eat. Daddy would have been looking forward to my visit so much and it must have really worried and hurt him to see my state of panic and distress. I was in no form to hold a conversation and after an awkward silence, I said I would go to my bed because I was wrecked from my journey.

That night as I lay awake, unable to sleep, I was so depressed, so frightened, and felt so worthless. In the morning, I did manage to have a cup of tea and toast and a brief conversation with Daddy before it was time to leave.

Eunan and his wife Nancy were driving me to Dublin and we drove the short distance to my mother's house for a brief visit. Like my Daddy, I knew Mammy was seriously worried about me, and although I was in no form for praying, I couldn't refuse when Mammy produced her Rosary beads and asked me to pray a decade with her, so as to keep us safe on our onwards journey. I was booked to return to London later that night and I promised my parents I would return soon for a proper visit.

My Horrors on a Jet Plane

Back on the road, I lay down across the back seat of the car, hoping I would sleep. I did manage to drift into a slumber for brief periods but once I awoke, my mind would be racing and playing havoc with me.

We arrived in good time for my first appointment in the Blackrock Clinic. The Blackrock Clinic is the leading and longest established private hospital clinic in Ireland. My appointment was with an urologist as I had told them I had lost all interest in sex as a result of my accident.

After waiting for ages, I finally got called in. The doctor examined all around my 'private area' and asked me all sorts of personal questions, which I knew I answered quite well. The doctor then produced a universal container and asked me for a sample of my sperm. As I was now preparing to give my sample, I was looking around the toilet to see if there were any cameras installed. I was taking my time and twisting up my face as if it was hurting me, just in case he was sitting watching my performance on a screen.

When I came out, Nancy asked how I got on. Even though I was still in really bad form, I still had my good sense of humour and told Nancy I was just like the 'wee genie' as I was after coming in a bottle as well!

As we made our way to my next appointment, we realised we were going to be late. Fitzwilliam Square was at least a twenty-five minute drive and we now found ourselves caught up in rush hour traffic, which made it much more frustrating.

I don't know how late I was when we arrived at our destination and when I told the lady at the reception desk my name and the name of the doctor I was to see, she told me there was no such person. I explained that was the name that was on my letter and when she asked me for the letter, I realised I had left it with the receptionist in the Blackrock Clinic. I had figured that, as they were both acting on behalf of the insurance company, they were just trying to confuse me and see how I would react. She suggested that I should phone my solicitor to clarify the matter, but I told her that she should phone the Blackrock Clinic instead, as it would only cost her the price of a local call. When she told me not to tell her what to do, I snapped back by saying, "Stop messing me about". She told me she wasn't going to listen while I was swearing at her and began walking briskly down a corridor, with me following in hot pursuit. She passed an open door and pointed towards it, signalling for me to enter. I was halfway in the door when a man, who looked near retiring age, shouted at me to close the door behind me. I shouted back, "Wait until I get in first". At this stage I was just totally shattered and was about to explode.

The doctor introduced himself and after getting off to a very bad start, our meeting then went completely out of control. Anything he said, I disagreed with, as I thought he was totally wrong. He then showed me all the letters after his name and asked who the hell I thought I was to be contradicting him.

"Do you think I am just an odd job man? I know what I am talking about," he said.

Well, I replied by telling him I also knew what he was talking about and it was just a load of bullshit. He removed his glasses and hit the table a thump with his fist and roared at me to get out. I was tempted to take a swing at him but I was so exhausted, both physically and mentally, that I would probably just have dropped at his feet.

In his report to my solicitor, he said that I was very aggressive and suggested I should be referred to a psychiatrist. My solicitor said the referral to the shrink might work out in my favour, since it could be argued that my aggression was a direct result of my accident.

Going Back to London

I decided to return to London and my solicitor also told me it was quite possible that the insurance company might have a private investigator follow and film my movements in London. That thought had crossed my mind previously. Although my antics would certainly have made amusing and damning footage, I tried to put it out of my mind and hope for the best.

One day, after cashing my disability benefit cheque, I was walking up the street and got caught in a fierce stormy shower. Since I was wearing a short sleeve shirt, I put my head down and started to run as fast as I could. The street was packed with people and I couldn't believe my luck when I collided with my doctor outside his surgery and almost knocked him to the ground. I just kept on running and didn't even take the time to apologise.

Back at the house, I knew I was in a predicament. How could I look for another sick cert? I was using my leg injury as my main reason for being unable to work. After thinking about it for a few minutes, I rang the surgery and asked the girl at reception for an appointment. I explained that it was very urgent and that I was in an awful lot of pain. She told me she had a cancellation and that I should just come on down. When the time came to face the music, I put on my 'poor me' act. I limped in through the door, letting out a few screeches to indicate that I was in severe agony.

Straight away my doctor asked if it was me that had run into him earlier. I said, "Maybe it was," and continued on by telling him that I was out for a walk and when the rain started, I was rushing back to the house and when I was almost at the top of the stairs, my legs just went numb and gave way. I explained that I had fallen down the stairs and needed some painkillers or an injection as my back was killing me.

He was reluctant at the outset to give me anything, but after a lot of persuasion I managed to get a prescription and another sick cert for one more month. When I moved into my lodgings, I thought it was great to be so close to the surgery but now I wasn't so sure. I knew that I would have trouble getting another cert from him, so I figured that I needed to change my doctor pretty soon.

Most of my hard drinking buddies were also claiming disability benefits, so the very next week I was introduced to a very good doctor and got registered at his surgery. He had a great understanding for my situation and said he would have no problem in declaring me unfit for work. It was a huge relief knowing that I didn't have to go back to my own doctor again.

When I was due my next cert, my new doctor asked how long I needed it for, so I told him that three months would do me for now. He gave it to me without any hesitation.

Pete arrived at my house one morning with two bottles of cider and six cans of extra strength lager. That was my first time getting introduced to snakebites. That morning after our breakfast of snakebites, I figured that if we got on the 266 bus, which passed my house, we could visit the Three Crowns pubs – the first one was in Harlesden, the second in Willesden and the third in Cricklewood.

That same night I was involved in another accident and miraculously escaped with my life. As Pete and myself were walking towards Cricklewood Broadway, I staggered out in front of an oncoming car and was thrown into the air. After picking myself up from the pavement, I realised I hadn't suffered any injuries and Pete and myself continued on walking as if nothing had happened. Needless to say the car never stopped.

Some days afterwards, I was craving a drink but didn't have any money. I decided I would go into the Windmill pub and ask Amy for a sub. When Amy asked me how much I wanted, I said I would need £50.

Amy said, "If I give you £50 now you won't bother looking for work tomorrow." She handed me £25 and told me to return the following day for the final instalment. But I said to her, "Amy, if you don't give me the £50 now, I will have to come back tomorrow for the rest of the money," to which she replied, "I suppose you're right," and she then handed me another £25.

I thanked Amy and told her I would pay her back as soon as I could. "I know I can trust you," she said, "Otherwise I wouldn't have given it to you".

Shortly after that, Bob, one of the regular lads at our local, asked if I was interested in getting a job in Southend-on-Sea, a seaside resort in Essex, about 40 miles from London. I could get picked up and dropped off each day by the works van at a café within walking distance to my house. The work would be heavy but well paid. I would get £65 a day and plenty of overtime if I wanted.

Well, I did start on that job and the first two weeks were tight going. My tools were a pick and shovel and my hands blistered after the first day, but once I got into my third week, I was okay and was able to hold my own. I managed to get my debt repaid to Joe and Amy.

We worked half days on Saturdays, so a group of us would always go to the pub on our way home for a few drinks. We always had the good intentions of going home and coming back out again, all prepared for a good night on the town. One Saturday we were in the pub, as usual, in our working gear, enjoying our drinks, when a lady, who was seated at a table with her girlfriends, caught my eye. I was very attracted to her, so after we exchanged eye contact, I approached her.

I planned my chat up line and went straight for it saying, "If I went home, had a shower and a shave, put on a nice aftershave, gelled my hair and put on my best clothes and came back and asked you out, what would you say?"

She laughed and said, "Yes, I would definitely go out with you.".

We exchanged first names and I told Beatrice I would be back very soon, after my makeover for our date. When I went back to the bar to finish my drink, I realised there were another four drinks waiting for me, so being an alcoholic I swallowed them one after the other in very quick succession. I then figured I couldn't leave without buying my round, so I ordered one for the road. As much as I needed to go home for my shower and change of clothes, I just couldn't leave my drink, so I decided I would approach Beatrice again and tell her there was a change of plan.

This time I said to her, "What if I didn't bother going home and asked you out. What would your answer be?"

She said her answer would still be the same and suggested I bring over my drink and join her at the table. During our conversation, I asked Beatrice what she was doing tomorrow, and when she asked me why I wanted to know, I said if she was free, I would like to meet her for a drink. Beatrice then told me that if I played my cards right I might end up beside her in the morning.

That night, Beatrice brought me back to her apartment in Chiswick, west London. It was around this time in my life that I started to develop a very weak bladder. To piss in one's own bed while sleeping alone was bad enough, but to piss in the bed belonging to a beautiful lady friend, whom you were just after meeting, was very embarrassing and not a very good start to any possible relationship.

Needless to say, we awoke on Sunday morning, and both of us was soaked in urine. I had pissed the bed big time. Neither of us mentioned it, and while Beatrice was having a well-earned shower, I decided to pop out to see if I could find an off-licence or a pub –

whichever came first. After walking down a few streets, I found a pub, so after I had four double vodkas inside me, I was ready to go back to my friend's house. But what I didn't remember to do was to check Beatrice's address before I left. So I'm sad to say, I never did make it back to see my friend. I remembered the house had a white door and a cat sitting outside. So for the next half hour or so, I must have counted at least half-a-dozen white doors and ten different cats as I desperately tried without success to locate Beatrice's house.

I made my way back to Acton and after a quick shower and change of clothes I went down to my local. I was figuring Pete would be there. After having a few drinks there, myself and Pete then got a taxi up to the Mean Fiddler pub in Harlesden, north-west London, where we knew there would be a live band playing until 3pm. That was the place to be on a Sunday for the craic back then.

After leaving the Fiddler shortly after 3pm, we somehow managed to lose each other in the crowd. Pete had recently moved to a new address in Ealing, and into a house that was also renowned for parties, so I decided I would make my way there with the hope of meeting him again. We just seemed to both arrive at the same time despite taking different routes back. You would think we were long lost brothers who hadn't seen each other in years as we were both delighted to be reunited.

There were two girls in the house so we asked them if they would like to join us for a drink. They accepted, so the four of us went to a pub of their choosing. Everything was going well until the band started playing and Pete and I got so high, we started dancing on the tables and chairs. We were asked to leave and it was only then that we realised that our lady friends had disappeared.

Standing outside the door considering our options, we both decided we would get a taxi and go to the National nightclub in Kilburn, north-west London. It would have a band playing and we knew it stayed open late. We also figured that our two lady friends might be there. But what we didn't think about was their strict dress code. Pete got stopped at the door by the bouncers as he was wearing runners.

We were both gutted as we could hear the music blaring and we were also craving more drink. As we walked down the street, feeling very sorry for ourselves, I noticed a wino sitting on the footpath wearing a pair of brown shoes that must have been at least a size 13. I approached him and, after explaining our situation, I asked him if he would sell us his shoes. He said he would need £5 as well as Pete's runners to do a deal. But once we got his shoes on Pete's feet, Pete took off running up the street carrying his runners in both hands. I soon followed with the wino in hot pursuit in his bare feet. As we raced up Kilburn High Road, I could hear the wino shouting, "Come back and honour your side of the deal you pair of thieves".

We did manage to escape, and gain entry into the National, but not for very long. While we waited on our two pints Pete turned to me and said, "Look at the size of my two big feet! I'll never get a woman in here tonight!"

I replied "You know what the women say about men with big feet".

Our sides were sore from laughing and instead of just drinking our pints and behaving ourselves, we tipped the pints into each runner which Pete had placed on the bar counter. We then continued by hitting our two empty glasses together, shouting cheers. But after that stunt we were both manhandled out the door by the bouncers, who had already been keeping a close eye on us. As well as Pete losing his runners, which had cost him £70, we were both barred from future admission to the National. I suppose we got what we deserved for stealing the wino's shoes.

I never bothered going to work on Monday and, as I assumed I would probably be sacked anyway, I decided I would take the rest of the week off. On Thursday I went up to the café to meet Bob, who had my wage packet, and Denis, my foreman, was also there. Denis looked at me for a few moments and then asked, "Where were you all week?" I told him I was away on the beer. He told me that he had sacked men for missing just one day but he was prepared to give me a second chance. He asked if I would come back in the morning and also work Saturday and Sunday to make up my wages.

I started back the next morning with the good intentions of keeping straight, but on the Saturday evening after work, I went out on the town and ended up at another house party. I went into work on Sunday morning, but told Denis I was shattered and too hung over to stay on. Denis suggested that if I stayed, I could go for a cure at lunchtime. So I did. Denis joined me for a drink and when he told me he was from Glasgow, I told him that was a coincidence as my two friends, whose house I was partying in the previous night, were also from Glasgow. He told me to take the two lads out with me in the morning and he would give them a start on the job. I said, 'There's only one problem, Denis, they are both women!' He laughed at that and then asked if I was sleeping with them, I said, "I wish I was".

Three weeks later, I was still in the same job, when I received a letter notifying me of an appointment in Dublin for the following Tuesday at 11am. The appointment was with a psychiatrist, who was going to assess me on behalf of the insurance company.

After another weekend of heavy drinking I didn't bother going to work. Once again I was just shattered and a bundle of nerves. I was now dreading my journey home, so I rang my doctor and arranged an appointment for later that same day. When he saw the state I was in, he wanted to admit me immediately to a detox unit, but I explained that I had to be in Dublin the following day and I needed something to calm my nerves. I told him about my previous experience, going into the horrors while travelling and that I was frightened it would happen to me again. Thankfully, he prescribed some tablets for me, and made me promise that once I returned to London I would seek help for my alcoholism.

After collecting my prescription, I took double my prescribed dosage and hoped for the best. Even though I knew I had enough money for my return ticket, I decided to phone my mate Leo and get a sub from him as I wanted to be on the safe side. After meeting with Leo and getting £250 I went into a travel agent's and booked my return flight. I figured it would be best to return the same day, because I was in no form to spend a night in Dublin.

I was very tempted to go for a drink, but decided I would go back to my room and wait and see if the tablets would make me feel any better. Back in my room, I was sitting on the edge of the bed, soaking in my own sweat and the tablets still hadn't made me feel any better. My mate, Bob, then arrived at my bedroom door and I knew by looking at him that he was also suffering from the horrors.

He asked me if I would come with him for a drink but I told him I was afraid to go drinking as I had to go to Dublin in the morning. I told him about my visit to the doctor and he asked if I would give him a few tablets and he would just go home and go to bed. I made the mistake of handing Bob the whole jar and I nearly passed out when he emptied out a handful and swallowed them.

I was in bad enough shape myself before that happened, but now I was feeling ten times worse. As well as getting robbed of most of my tablets, I was now worrying that Bob might have overdosed. As he was walking out the door, he told me to phone him in the morning and he would come to Dublin with me for the craic. What made matters even worse was the fact that Bob was driving his own motorbike, a powerful 1000cc. The speed he took off up Horn Lane, I never thought he would make it home in one piece. But thank God he did.

After I counted what tablets I had left, I took a few more and lay down on top of my bed, dreading the night ahead. As well as

Going Back to London

feeling really frightened, I also felt so alone and wished I was at home with my family, where I knew I would be safe. Also I had wet my bed a few nights previously and this added to my discomfort and paranoia.

After tossing and turning and raving throughout the night I got up early in the morning to face the day ahead. By this stage I had no tablets left either so in sheer desperation I said to myself, "I need a drink". I didn't have too far to walk to an off-licence, which I knew would be opened early, so after buying a bottle of whiskey, I booked a taxi for Heathrow airport to pick me up an hour later. I never bothered phoning Bob that morning and before my taxi arrived I was in such good form, I would have been happy to fly anywhere in the world.

I consumed more drink in the airport bar and somehow I managed to make it to Dublin that day for my appointment but my memory of it is next to none. I could quite easily have overdosed with the amount of tablets and drink combined. The appointment with my psychiatrist must have passed off without incident. I'm sure he would have known that, as I was a chronic alcoholic, it was senseless even to try to have a conversation with me that day. I don't have any recollection whatsoever of my return flight back to London and it's amazing how I managed to get through security. Although Denis had told me to call him when I returned from Dublin, I never did.

Myself and Pete would sometimes just hop on a bus or tube and randomly get off and start drinking in whatever area we found ourselves. We were always trying to dodge paying the correct fares and quite often we wouldn't purchase a ticket at all, depending on our financial situation. We had many crazy escapades as a result. Although there was a substantial penalty should you get arrested and prosecuted for such an offence, it didn't deter us as we continued playing cat and mouse games with the ticket collectors and inspectors of London transport.

One day we found ourselves walking up a street in Peckham, south-east London There was a large rocking chair on display outside a furniture shop and without speaking Pete lifted it and rested it on his shoulder and continued on walking. I was almost certain we had got away unnoticed, as we seemed to be walking for ages. We were taking it in turns to carry it, but when a van pulled up beside us and four men jumped out we knew we were in trouble. The owner of the shop told us in an firm manner that if we didn't hand over the chair he would have no hesitation in having us both shot. We soon left down the chair after that and, even though I could picture the chair in my living room, we figured it wasn't worth getting shot over.

Later, in a bar, we befriended a lady named Joanne and she told us we could stay at her place for the night. We bought a carry-out of drink and we ended up crashing out on Joanne's living room floor.

When I awoke early the following morning, my body was all aches and pains and I was also shivering with the cold. There was a bottle of whiskey and a bottle of vodka beside us. I asked Joanne, whom I assumed owned the flat, to put the kettle on as I was looking forward to having a hot whiskey. Joanne then informed me that was not possible as we were in a squat and the electricity had been disconnected.

After drinking our bottles straight, the three of us then went drinking around a few different bars in the Peckham area. That night we ended up in the Archway Tavern on Holloway Road, north London. Everything was going well until it was time to leave. We hailed a taxi and Pete got in the front while Joanne and I got in the back. Just as the taxi was about to move off, another man, whom I had not seen before, jumped in and sat at the other side of Joanne.

We had been travelling in silence for a distance when I felt compelled to sing a song. I knew I was not a very good singer but, when our 'unknown' passenger told me to shut my mouth, I took offence and asked him if he was looking for a fight. When he said that he was, the taxi driver stopped abruptly and told us all to get out.

Myself and my fighting partner started exchanging punches and by now were out in the middle of a busy street. I was coming under pressure, so my mate Pete came to my rescue and hit my opponent a powerful uppercut, which knocked him to the ground. Pete then put his big arm around my shoulder and said, "We had to go for a knockout".

By now the police had arrived on the scene, and our opponent was still lying knocked out on the pavement. Joanne came to our rescue, and told the policemen that our victim had actually attacked her. Joanne also admitted hitting him over the head with her high-heeled shoes. An ambulance came and transferred our sparring partner to hospital and, after arresting Pete, Joanne and me, the police placed us in the back of the paddy wagon, and took us to the police station. They locked us up in separate cells for the night. The next day we were released at different times. When it was my turn to get out I asked the policeman where I was. He informed me that we were in King's Cross, central London. We were lucky we were not charged for that incident, and I made my way back to Acton alone.

One Sunday morning I decided I would go down to the Windmill for a drink as I knew I would meet a lot of my mates. During the course of the day, I got talking to a fellow I had never met before, so I included him in my round and bought him a pint (for the purposes of this story we shall refer to him as Matt, as I didn't get his name). It was normal on a Sunday to get into rounds. So on that particular day there was a large group of men in the same company, and every time someone bought a round they included Matt as they assumed he was a mate of mine.

After being bought a large amount of drink, Matt then asked me for a sub of £10. He explained that he had just come in for a few quiet pints and hadn't been prepared for joining company and buying rounds. Once he got his £10 from me, he said he would then have enough money to buy his round and that he would square me up again. He also asked to keep our transaction a secret.

After I passed him the £10 he still made no attempt to buy a drink. Then one of the lads in our company asked me, "What kind of a user is that you're with?" I told him I didn't know him and had only met him for the first time that morning. As well as not buying a drink, Matt started slagging off our county football team. I knew then that I was going to confront him, but as I didn't want to cause any trouble, out of my respect for the landlady, I suggested to Matt that we would go next door to the Blarney Stone pub for a pint.

I also decided I would take my drink with me to make sure that Matt would have to buy his own. As we both made our way next door we didn't speak, and once inside I walked over to a table and sat down with my precious drink (a double brandy). When Matt joined me, empty handed, I couldn't help but say, "Is it not time you were buying a drink?" Matt flew into a rage and pulled a bundle of money from his pocket and said, "I could buy all the drink in the bar if I wanted to". He was now towering over me, so once I apologised and got him settled and seated, I hit him a thump that knocked him off his chair and across the floor. I assumed I would be barred, so I swallowed my drink and walked out.

Back in the Windmill, I discovered my friend, Matt, had got £10 from at least six other men in my company. What I also discovered was that I didn't get barred from the Blarney Stone. When I did venture in again I apologised to the landlord. He said to me, "I'm sorry as well that you didn't hit him half hard enough".

My solicitor rang and said that all was going well with my case and it would be finalised within the next three months or so. Edmund was coping much better than I was in the 'Big Smoke' and had been in the same job for sometime and told me he would ask Leo to send me there. Things were looking good for me once again.

Going Back to London

I now thought I had everything figured out. I would go to work with Edmund, ease up on my drinking and once I received my compensation, I would come back home and settle down. Little did I know that this was going to be my last job in England.

The job was in Newbury, a town located in Berkshire, south-east England and was 52 miles from London. We would get picked up outside the office in Shepherds Bush each morning and several vans would then travel out together, since there was a large body of men employed. It was good fun coming home each evening, as the drivers would all race each other. However, they never seemed to be in the same panic in the morning.

I had suggested to Leo that he should keep some money out of my wages each week as I wanted to repay my debt. But he never did. Edmund took me under his wing and on my first day he introduced me to all the lads on the job as the 'wee brother'. I was then told I would be working alongside Edmund. If I had been paired off with a stranger I would not have survived my first day. Edmund was in good form at the time, so he took care of any heavy lifting or anything that was a bit tricky for me. I remember thinking to myself on my first day that I was in 'quare' bad shape. I knew that if I could get the first week over and stay sober that I would get broken in again and become fitter and more able. Once I got my first pay packet. I went away on another bender and missed the following week's work.

Edmund did manage to track me down and urged me to return to work, so I decided I would give it another go. There were several pubs located close to the job, so every chance I got I would sneak into one and swallow a few double brandys. With the amount of drink I was consuming, I was a danger to myself and anyone else who was near me.

One day, when I was both drunk and in the horrors, I fell down a hole in the roof which was for erecting a lift shaft. Ironically, I had earlier been given the responsibility of making it safe. I fell twelve feet onto hard concrete and landed on my back. I landed beside a work colleague who got such a fright that he just ran away without waiting to attend to me. Edmund and several other lads on the job rushed to my aid, and with their assistance I managed to make it into the passenger seat of the works van. I was in sheer agony and worried that I might have suffered serious injury. Jack, our foreman, then insisted on taking me to a nearby hospital, but as I was claiming benefits I didn't want to go, because I was concerned they might put two and two together.

After a lot of persuasion, Jack did agree to take me to a hospital in Acton and I told the doctors there that I had fallen down the stairs in my house. I was pleased when my x-ray revealed that I hadn't broken any bones, but I did suffer severe bruising to my back and legs. I spent the next three weeks on crutches, and as I was trying to adjust to my circumstances, I felt very alone and vulnerable at times. The thought of my compensation claim being finalised and returning to the security of my own home was the light at the end of this dark tunnel in which I found myself.

I was back walking without my crutches and, once again, Edmund asked me would I like to start back at work in Newbury, as the job was near completion. I thought it would be nice to see some of the lads again.

On my first day back Jack showed me a large flat roof, which, he told me, had to be painted. I would be working with a fellow from Greece. I had been hoping he would send me with Edmund or some of my mates with whom I could have the craic. I tried talking to the Greek, but he couldn't understand a word I was saying. I thought to myself, "I'm not going to spend a few days up here with you." It was also the same roof I had fallen through, so my heart was not too bothered about doing a good job and I was also craving for a drink.

I noticed a large sweeping brush so I made a plan. The paint was stacked in five gallon containers. I started emptying the paint onto the roof in different places. I then got hold of the sweeping brush and started levelling it out. I was working at a furious rate. The Greek approached me with his hands flying in the air, indicating for me to stop, but I ignored him and reached for another container of paint.

He was now standing in front of me in protest. I told him to get out of my way. When he ignored me, I emptied some paint over his feet. That changed his mind and as he tried to run away from me, I followed him, throwing out large puddles of paint. Two agents then arrived up beside me on the roof. I was busy with my sweeping and they just stared at me in disbelief. As well as painting the Greek's shoes, I had also covered tiles, timbers and part of a skylight. One of the agents remarked that I was doing a fine job, so I thought one sarcastic remark deserved another! I replied, "My brush is a bit on the small side". I then fired my brush into a skip that was sitting on the ground below and walked off the job in search of a drink.

It was also around this time that I lost my two anonymous friends' social security cheques that I had been cashing. At 9am one morning, I answered the phone to some gentleman who had said he wanted to speak with a Mr. so and so. I was caught unawares and told him he didn't live there anymore. It was when he asked to whom he was speaking that I became suspicious and hung up the phone. When the phone rang the following morning at the same time, I recognised his voice. This time he said he was looking for a Miss so and so, who he said was an old college friend. I told him I would check her room to see if she was in and a short moment later I told the caller that she had just gone out. Later that same day, two officers from the local Social Security office visited our house to carry out investigations on housing benefit claims. As a result I lost a great wee source of income, but was very lucky they didn't follow up on their investigations and look to prosecute those responsible for benefit fraud.

After that, things just seemed to go from bad to worse and I never bothered looking for another job. One night, after getting involved in another brawl, I got clobbered over the head with a plank of timber, needing seven stitches to a nasty wound on my head as a result.

On another occasion I was asked to leave a bar when two men in my company started fighting. I left, assuming I wasn't barred as I hadn't been involved in the row. When I ventured in the next morning, I was both shocked and annoyed when I was told I was indeed barred. I was really hung over and left without any fuss as I needed a drink. I drank all day in another bar and couldn't stop thinking about my unfair barring and thought I should go back in and confront the landlord. Once inside, I immediately started smashing up the place and in the space of a moment or so I had broken two windows and a large mirror. The bar was packed with customers and in that moment of sheer madness, I also pulled a large chandelier from the ceiling. It went crashing down on a group of men playing cards at a table. I just about managed to make my escape through an exit door when the landlord, armed with a baton, and several annoyed customers came racing at me. I ran down several side streets until I arrived at a hotel. I went in and booked myself a room, because I knew I had to get off the streets. As I sat on my bed waiting on the night porter to bring me a drink, I could hear the police sirens sounding in the distance and wondered were they looking for me.

My £90,000 Compensation

My solicitor rang and informed me that the insurance company had made us an offer of £90,000. They would also pay all legal costs, as well as my hospital bills, which amounted to £24,000. It was their third and final offer. We could go into court but there was no guarantee we would get any more. There was also the danger of getting less. Since I wasn't in permanent employment before my accident, I couldn't claim loss of earnings. It was also pointed out to me that I had a high amount of alcohol consumed, meaning that I was partly to blame. We accepted their offer and my solicitor told me my cheque would be available for collecting in his office in a few days' time.

I approached Leo again for another sub of £250 as I didn't have enough money for the fare home. I now owed Leo £500, and told him that when I received my compensation, I would pay him back. Coincidentally, the day I received my cheque, 3rd May, 1990 was my twenty-seventh birthday. As it would take a few days for the cheque to clear, I borrowed £200 from my solicitor as I wanted to celebrate and have a good drink for my birthday. After paying off any debts I had at home, and dividing out £5,000 between my family members (Edmund had also moved home and was living at our mother's house), I once again headed back to London and my room was still available in Horn Lane.

I was anxious to get my debt repaid to Leo, so I rang and arranged to meet him at his office. Leo advised me to go back to work but all I wanted that morning was another drink. Being an alcoholic and craving drink with so much money in my possession, you must understand that going back to work that day was the last thing on my mind. I shook hands with Leo and thanked him for his kindness, as I turned to walk away I could see Leo looking anxiously at me and I thought I could sense a tint of sadness in his eyes. Leo would have seen the bigger picture.

I don't know what possessed me to continue on staying in London but that was what I did. I suppose it was my selfish attitude as I didn't have anyone waiting on me or asking me questions.

I was now on a continuous bender in London. I can't remember what the exchange rate was for converting punts into sterling, but I was aware I was blowing a huge amount of my compensation money that could have been better used on my family at home. Deep down I was thinking that tomorrow would be different – I would get sober, and get my priorities in order, move home and settle down.

One morning, after drinking a bottle of vodka in my digs, I decided, on the spur of a moment, that I was going home. I phoned my mom's house and also talked to my father, who said he was glad I was coming home. He said we would go to the bog together the following morning.

I was genuinely looking forward to seeing my family again. I never bothered packing a bag and a few hours later I was having a drink in Dublin city centre. Although I was aware of the time the bus was leaving for Donegal, I didn't give myself enough time for the short walk and when I realised I had missed my bus I took the crazy decision of going back out to Dublin airport. I don't know what came over me, but I booked another flight back into London.

The next morning I rang home again and explained that I was still in London and had been offered a handy wee job and had decided to give it a go and get my life back on track. I suppose I was trying to reassure my parents that I was ok and to justify my reasons for remaining in London. Deep down, I was also trying to reassure myself, but I continued on my bender and there were some days when I would consume three bottles of spirits and still remember everything. I also had the habit of changing my drinks. Sometimes I would do binges on brandy, vodka or whiskey. If I was in really bad form, I would start the day drinking brandy or port, or, if I was feeling cold, I would start drinking hot whiskey.

It was around this time that I decided to move out of Horn Lane. I knew I was on a downward spiral and I assumed a change of address would be enough to inspire me to make a new start and get my life sorted. I cancelled my claim for rent allowance and disability benefit and moved into a well-maintained house in North Kensington, west London, convenient for Central line, Hammersmith line and City line tube stations and fifteen minutes by tube to central London.

On the morning I moved into my new digs, I rang my sister Bridie with my new address and phone number. Later that same day, when I was checking out the tubes and buses, I realised I had not kept a copy of the address myself. I couldn't remember it so I had to phone Bridie again and ask her where I was living. After that I made sure I wrote it down.

I fully intended going back to work but my craving for drink was so strong I continued on my bender. Although I was still missing Mass, I would always say a few prayers to St Anthony on a daily basis asking for his protection, because I knew I was living life on the edge.

Meeting Karen

A few weeks after I had moved into my new lodgings, I found myself drinking back in Acton with my mate Paul. It was about 8pm and we were walking up Churchfield Road and both of us were well steamed. I noticed a girl walking down the other side of the street, so I called over and asked if she would like to join us for a drink. She was wearing earphones so she crossed over to our side. As she removed her earphones, Paul took a back step as he was certain she was going to thump me one. I asked her again if she would like to join me for a drink and, to our surprise, she replied, "Sure, let's go" and she told us her name was Gina. The three of us then walked the short distance to the Windmill pub.

The drinks were coming up fast and furious and I was putting them away as quickly as the barman was handing them to me. Needless to say, I soon forgot about Gina, but my mate Paul didn't and he later walked her home.

The next morning I awoke, and figuring Paul would not be at work, I called a taxi to take me to his house. I wanted a mate to go on a session with. When I got into the house Paul was already on the phone to his new woman. She told Paul she would meet him at 1pm, in exactly the same place where I had called her over the previous night. She told Paul to bring me with him as she had a real nice friend for me. Paul was all business but all I wanted that morning was more drink.

After getting the cure, we made our way to the arranged location, and sure enough the two girls were waiting for us. After getting introduced to Karen I thought I wouldn't have a hope in hell with her. I really fancied her and thought to myself that she could have any man she wanted. But I decided I would chance my arm and ask her out. I thought, she will refuse and then I'll be free to go back to the pub and have a good drink! But when Karen said yes, I was both surprised and delighted.

Karen was from the north-east of England, Newcastle to be precise. She had moved down to London and was now working as a live-in child-minder. She had to be back in her house by 10pm each weekday night but had her weekends free.

Our first week went very well. We met every day at lunchtime and we would go to the park with the two children she was taking care off. Karen was free each evening after 6pm, so we would meet again and spend four hours together before she had to go home.

The first weekend we were together I took Karen on a tour of the bars and clubs. The following Tuesday lunchtime, I told Karen that I had to go and meet with a man who was giving me a job, but Karen was not going to be fooled so easily, and she told me she knew I was just going to the pub. So, with that, I invited her to join me. Karen said she couldn't as she had the two children with her, but I told her it wouldn't be a problem as I knew a pub where we could go for a few quiet drinks where nobody would bother us.

We were still there at 6 pm when Karen was due to finish for the evening, so we ordered a taxi to take us all back to Karen's place. At that time, I would have thought it was normal to go drinking during the day and wouldn't have realised how serious it was to bring Karen and the two children into the bar with me. I waited for Karen in the taxi as she took the children inside. Once she had that sorted, I figured we could go and enjoy a good drink.

It wasn't long until I heard a man's voice shouting in anger and the next thing I know, Karen's belongings are flying out onto the street in black bin-liners. I asked the taxi driver to wait for me so that I could go and see if Karen was okay.

When Karen's boss saw me walking up his footpath, he screamed at me, "Get off my property," and said that he was going to call the police. Once I realised Karen was safe, I gathered up her belongings and put them in our taxi. It was a bad situation. As well as Karen losing her job, she now had no place to stay, so I asked her if she wanted to move in with me until she got herself sorted. I felt guilty and knew it was all my fault.

Although we had only met each other the previous week, we now found ourselves living together. Karen suggested that we'd both look for work, as we couldn't continue drinking and dossing about. Karen did apply for several jobs but I just couldn't get motivated or sober.

One day I suggested to Karen we would go up to north London. I had a few mates living there whom I hadn't seen for some time. We met up with them in a bar on Holloway Road and, needless to say, we all had a good session. After agreeing a price with a mini cab driver, Karen and myself set off on our journey back to North Kensington.

When we were about two thirds of the way into our journey, I noticed the meter had already reached the fare we had agreed on, so I confronted the driver and asked what he was playing at. When I told him he wasn't getting a penny more than the price we had agreed, he stopped the taxi suddenly, got out of the car and opened the boot. I thought to myself that he must have a weapon in there, so I decide to throw myself at him and I threw a few punches. We were fighting in the middle of the street and we were disrupting the traffic, and all I could hear were horns blowing and people shouting at us. It was at this stage that Karen came to my rescue; she went to the open boot and found the length of timber the driver probably intended using on me. He must have figured then that he wasn't going to beat us both, so he made a run for it and hopped back into the car.

We still needed a lift, so I managed to get back in beside him and I held the handbrake until Karen got on board. The driver then told us we had two choices, "either pay the fare requested or I'll take

Meeting Karen

you to the police station". Before I got the chance to reply, Karen told him to take us to the police station if he wanted. I certainly didn't want to go anywhere near a police station, but Karen said, "Don't worry, honey, everything will be alright". Sure enough, the driver landed us at the station and he made a complaint against us for assault. Karen explained to the policeman that the driver had attempted to grope her and that I had stepped in to save her. When she was asked to make a statement, she said she would accept an apology if the driver withdrew his complaint against me. Needless to say, Karen, myself and the taxi man were relieved to get out of the police station without a case to answer.

I rang Leo and told him I was anxious to return to work and that I had also decided to go off the drink. Leo told me to call down to the office on Monday morning and he would have a job lined up for me.

My intentions were good. I now had my whole life figured out. I shared my great news with Karen and she was overjoyed. On Sunday morning I asked Karen if she fancied going for one last drink with me. Tomorrow I would go to work and we could look forward to our new life of sobriety and peace together. Karen also suggested that when she got herself a job, we would get ourselves a nice little flat away, somewhere private where we could be alone together.

I figured the Swakley Bar on Askew Road, Sheppard's Bush was as good a place as any for our last session. I knew it would have a live band playing until the first closing time at 3pm and I also knew I would meet a lot of friends there. We joined my old mate, Paul, and his girlfriend Gina.

Everything was going well until the barman called last orders and I now had an awful craving for more. After I bought a good round for my company, I then went back up to the bar and ordered ten more brandies for myself. The barman asked if I was sure and I replied, "Yes, keep them coming". I picked up two at a time and placed them neatly on an empty table. The table was round and I had them sitting neatly spaced out around the edge. I then said, "If anyone would like to join me for my last drink they should come quick as they won't be sitting around for too long".

I sat at the table on my own, and one after the other I swallowed the shorts down in quick succession. I went back up to Karen and explained that, as it was going to be my last session, I wanted it to be a good one! I then suggested we all go to a house party in Acton. The girls said they would give it a miss and Karen said she would meet me later back at our house.

On our way to the party we stopped at an off-license in East Acton and bought a bottle of brandy and a bottle of vodka. We were asked to leave the party when Paul thumped another guest, so we went up to another bar where I knew we could get a drink. We weren't long there when Paul took part in his second bout of the day, so once again we were asked to leave.

We figured by the time we got back down to the Swakley bar it would be open again for business. As we were walking down, or probably staggering down, Acton High Street to get a taxi, I suggested we would go into a Kentucky Fried Chicken café for a bite to eat.

Inside the café, Paul put a cigarette into his mouth and asked the other customers for a light. There were two men and two women sitting on high stools eating and one of them replied, "Sorry mate, we don't smoke". We were about to place our orders when the same gentleman took a packet of cigarettes from his pocket and passed them around his friends. Paul looked at me in disbelief, while the two men and two women were breaking their sides laughing at us. Paul and myself didn't think it was very funny and in the very next instant we punched the two men and knock them off their stools. As they fell to the floor, we had two angry women screaming at us so we decided we would make a run for it.

Meeting Karen

We had just gone down the street a little bit when we were grabbed by two policemen and were told that we were under arrest. Karen and Gina arrived on the scene at the same time as we were being put into the back of the paddy wagon. Karen asked one of the policemen what the hell was going on and he snapped back and told her to mind her own business. Karen said it was her business as she lived with me! So that really put the cat among the pigeons because, when the policeman asked our address, she gave it to him. But I had already given them the wrong address.

Karen insisted on coming to the police station with me. They put me in a cell on my own and I soon fell asleep. Paul was locked up on his own as well, in the cell next to me. When they brought me out in the morning they handed me a charge sheet stating they were releasing me on police bail. My true and loyal friend Karen was still there waiting for me.

As we made our way out of Acton police station that morning, we were both shivering from the cold. Someone had tipped over the rubbish bins, and we later discovered it was my mate, Paul, who had been released some time earlier.

It was too late now for me to report to my new job, and anyway I was in no form for work, so after getting ourselves some breakfast, we decided we would go back to our house and sleep it off. I don't know how long we were in bed but we were awoken by a racket outside. It was my old mate Pete and he was raving drunk. He must have thought I didn't want to see him as he was talking aloud to himself saying, "Now that he has got himself a woman, he doesn't want to know me".

I opened up the door and said, "Come on in you raving head case". He had one bottle of brandy for me and a bottle of vodka for himself. So much for my new start! Once Pete sat down, he fell asleep. I brought my brandy upstairs and sat on the side of the bed. I was completely shattered and my mind was racing. Karen was lying watching me and I knew she was worried and concerned and wondering where it would all end. I was supposed to be starting a new job, not drinking, and we were going to get our lives back on track. But instead I now found myself with a bottle of brandy in my hand and out on police bail. I put the bottle to my mouth. I drank about a quarter of it and then turned to Karen and said, "We need to get out of here".

When Karen asked where we would go, I said, "We will go to my home in Carrigart". I was so relieved when Karen said she would come with me. When Pete finally woke up, I had to break our news to him. Pete was gutted and said, "Don't break the partnership". He then suggested that the three of us should go to Manchester as he had friends there who would get us work and digs. I said I had my mind made up this time and if I got home safe and well I would "Never return again to this crazy city".

All I had to do now was to get through the night, so I asked Karen to walk with me to the off-licence. I was so weak and paranoid that Karen had to hold my hand like a baby as we crossed the busy street. Once again I bought two more bottles and Karen got enough groceries to make us all a good feed. I remember seeing the expression on Pete's face when we got back to the house with the carry out.

"You're going to kill us," he said. Karen made us all a good feed and with a struggle I managed to eat some. We continued on drinking through most of the night. The next morning, I ordered a taxi to take us to Heathrow, and suggested to Pete that he would be better off getting out of London and moving home. He was also from Ireland. At this stage Pete and I were both in the horrors and still drunk. Pete agreed with me and said he would go to Dublin as he had family living there.

As the three of us got into the taxi, Pete asked the driver to take him to his flat as he needed to collect his clothes and his tools. I told the taxi driver we didn't have time to be touring around London and he should take us straight to the airport. I turned around to Pete, who was sitting in the back, and said to him, "I'll buy you clothes and tools when we get to Dublin". I also told him that he was looking wild rough, to which he replied, "You don't look too smart yourself".

At Heathrow Airport, Pete bought a disposable shaving set and went to the toilet to shave. But with the shakes, he did more harm than good and his face was cut in several places. It was the first time I laughed that morning. Pete then declared that he had no ID with him and so couldn't come with us. I told him that I was both sad and glad to be leaving him! We shook hands and wished each other the best. I made my way to the ticket desk and bought Karen and myself two return tickets to Dublin. I bought the return tickets, in case I was stopped and questioned about skipping my bail.

Karen and myself arrived at my home and received a warm welcome from my father, who was awaiting our arrival. When I suggested to Daddy that we might need to buy another bed, he asked what the sleeping arrangements in London were. I told him we just used the one bed, so he said, "Well, sure the one will be enough for you here as well and there's no need to be putting extra expense on yourselves".

The house itself at that time was very basic, to say the least. We still didn't have a bathroom, nor running hot water, and our toilet was located in an outhouse that was known as our coalhouse. So it meant getting up and going out in the middle of the night if nature called. Our heating system consisted of an old range in the kitchen, which was also used for cooking. I hired a contractor to do some work on our home. Nothing fancy, but just the basics. We needed a bathroom, new doors and windows, and we really needed oil-fired central heating installed. The contractor quoted me a price of £15,000, which I thought was good. He explained he was very busy at that particular time but would get back to me at a later date.

This was a job I should have organised immediately on receiving my compensation. We didn't have a television either, so one day we went to Letterkenny and I ended up buying a fourteen-inch portable television, the cheapest one in the shop! Was that not crazy or what?

Karen seemed happy with our situation for a while. I always remember her singing and laughing around our house as she kept herself busy washing and scrubbing the place from top to bottom. In the meantime, we had a phone installed, which was good for Karen to keep in touch with family back at home.

Karen's Mom asked her if she would return home for a period and look after the house while she travelled with her work. Karen asked me to come with her to Newcastle, on the condition that I remain sober. She had been pleading with me to stop my binge drinking; otherwise, she said I was either going to kill myself or end up in prison. She had also threatened to end our relationship and only agreed to give me another chance when I promised to mend my ways.

Once again, I failed on my promise to Karen to get myself sorted, and after I went on a binge in Newcastle, Karen said she couldn't put up with me any longer and it was finally over between us. I was gutted and I knew I had only myself to blame. I decided once again that I would go home to Carrigart.

Although I had withdrawn a substantial amount from my bank prior to leaving for Newcastle, I realised I didn't have enough money on me for the fare. I rang my bank at home and told them to send £500 to Karen's address. Realising then that it could take a week or so for my cheque to arrive, I rang another mate called John, who was living and working in Leeds, and explained my predicament. John told me to get the bus down to Leeds and he would meet me.

Karen and I both cried our eyes out as we parted company that day at Newcastle bus station. I had just about enough for the bus fare, but knew I would be okay when I got to Leeds.

Meeting Karen

John met me at the station and gave me a good sub, so after another few days in Leeds, I finally made it home again to Donegal. I hadn't told Karen that I had ordered a cheque to her address, so I decided I was going to forget about it and let her keep it, as she had been so good and loyal to me. You can imagine my surprise when, three weeks later, I received a letter from Karen and my cheque enclosed. My bank had made a big mistake and the cheque was for £5,000 instead of £500. In her letter, Karen said she was sorry for not posting it sooner. She explained she didn't have the price of the stamp. Reading her letter, my eyes filled with tears and it took me several attempts to finally read its whole contents. She wished me peace and happiness in the future and it was obvious from reading between the lines that she didn't want me making contact with her again.

The contractors had now finished our renovations. I was lucky I had it done at that stage when I still had enough money to pay for it. I was gutted that Karen wasn't around now to see it and enjoy it.

Continuing to Live Life on the Edge

At home, my social life meant having to get a taxi to Letterkenny, or some other town, as I was still barred from most of the local pubs and clubs. It was costly and hard work trying to get a taxi for the return journey home.

One night, my mate Charlie and I were returning from a nightclub in Letterkenny. We were travelling in a taxi and I had purchased a bottle of whiskey. As we were going down the road, I decided we should stop off at another mate Daniel's house and spend the night there. I thought it would be handy for us in the morning, as we would be within walking distance of the pub. Then another brainwave hit me – I decided I would try and dodge paying the fare, thus ensuring I had more money for the following day. I kept this plan to myself, and I asked the driver to stop about six doors away from Daniel's house in a housing estate. I jumped out, carrying my bottle and ran off in between two houses. I knew Daniel's back door wouldn't be locked, so I ran as hard as I could through back gardens to my intended address. I could hear the commotion at the front of the houses between Charlie and the taxi driver. Charlie was calling out for me to return and pay the fare.

I was laughing as I ran in the back door and upstairs to the room in which I knew Daniel slept. But I soon stopped laughing when I realised I had gone into the wrong house. There was a couple in bed and I must admit I really gave them both a fright. The lady was screaming and the man was going to box me, but when I apologised and explained what had happened they were okay about it. In fact, they also had a good sense of humour and the three of us then watched out the bedroom window as Charlie and the driver both fell to the ground as they wrestled with each other. When the driver finally realised that he wasn't going to get paid, he left.

A few weeks after that incident, Charlie and myself were together again, drinking in a bar not far from Daniel's house. It was a Sunday morning and there was only one other customer present. Things were going well until Charlie and this character began to argue. The landlord told us he was closing up for a few hours as he had to cook the dinner. I thought it was a clever way of getting us out and avoiding a row.

Although there were five other bars in the town, we couldn't go into them since we were previously barred from all five. So I bought a bottle of whiskey and started walking down the street towards Daniel's house, laughing as I watched Charlie stagger down the opposite side of the street cursing and swearing out loud. As I was walking past the Garda barracks, I noticed the door was open, and on the spur of the moment I walked inside. I can't remember what was going through my mind at that particular moment but then I realised, "I'm standing inside a Garda Station that I have no reason whatsoever to be in, with a bottle of whiskey in my hand".

I didn't see any Gardaí and it was all very quiet. It was then that I noticed the uniforms. Without another thought, I put on the Garda hat and coat and walked back out again onto the street, where I could feel people looking at me. At this stage I was swigging out of my bottle and was anxious to get to Daniel's house, before I got myself arrested, so I decided I needed a taxi.

I walked in the door of what I believed was the taxi driver's house, and once again I discovered I had made the same mistake as before and was in the wrong house. I was met by a woman who could not believe what she was seeing. Here I was, dressed as a Garda, staggering and drinking from a bottle of whiskey. I told her, "I'm the new Sheriff in town and I believe you have poitin in your house."

She was breaking her sides laughing at me and replied, "Honestly Guard, I have no poitin".

I then replied, "Well, in that case you might as well have a drink of my whiskey".

By that stage both of us were in stitches. I then went next door to the taxi driver's house. He looked at me from head to toe before agreeing to take me to Daniel's house. As we were travelling up the street, I spotted my mate Charlie driving a tractor, which he must have borrowed without the owner's permission, so I asked my taxi driver to stop immediately as "I want to get out and make an arrest."

I jumped out, stood in front of the approaching tractor and signalled for Charlie to stop. I should have known Charlie better, as the next thing I know, he is increasing his speed and is driving straight for me. I was lucky to be just about sober enough to jump out of his way! I watched then as Charlie disappeared around a corner, driving on the wrong side of the road before walking the short distance to Daniel's house.

Instead of taking the time to open the gate, I just climbed over the wooden fence and went to the kitchen window and knocked on it. When Daniel's wife saw me, she asked him, "What did you do last night? There's a Garda out there!"

When they realised it was actually me, I received a warm welcome. Inside the house, I removed my uniform. It didn't take us long to finish the bottle of whiskey, so once again I made my way back into town in search of another bottle. I left the uniform in the house. I met a fellow on the street whom I knew, so after giving him the money, he got me another bottle of whiskey from a pub I was barred from. I was now on my journey back to Daniel's house.

Now, the first time I went into the barracks, it was just a spur of the moment decision, but as I passed for the second time, I decided to chance my luck again. I went in, got another uniform, and came out wearing it. I managed to make it up to Daniel's house again, but I eventually landed back down in the town creating mayhem. I had been in a few bars telling them to close, before trying to operate check points outside on the street. It was at this stage that I finally got arrested.

When Daniel heard I was locked up in the station he arrived with the first uniform and gave it back. He assumed it would help my case. The Garda at the desk asked him, "Is there any more of our property in your house?" To which Daniel replied, "Why, are you missing much more?" I suppose at that stage nobody knew for certain what I had got away with.

One day I went up to visit my mother and as I was walking up the street I saw a traveller man rushing out the door, and Edmund in hot pursuit. Occasionally back then traveller people might visit your house offering to sell something or maybe just ask for a donation of some sort. What made this particular incident so funny was the fact that Edmund was completely naked. Edmund always slept in the nude and when he heard the traveller talking in a raised voice he hopped out of bed, and launched his attack. As the traveller was running towards me, Edmund shouted, "Grab hold of him while I go in and put on my boots". I could only laugh as the traveller sped past me at such speed that he could have given a race horse a good run for his money.

Sometime after that incident, I found myself drinking alone in a bar and a tinker man came in and we struck up a conversation. I asked him to join me for a drink and some hours later we were both in good form, enjoying each other's character and exchanging rounds of drinks. My new drinking buddy asked me to excuse him while he went out to his van and promised he would be back in a few minutes. True enough, he returned and presented me with a large 'pandy', which tinker men were renowned and gifted in making. A 'pandy' is a container made from tin and was mainly used by farmers for holding the milk whilst milking their cows. My 'pandy' was skilfully crafted complete with its own handle. Although I had no plans for taking up any farming chores, I thanked my friend for his gift and immediately I emptied my drink into it and proceeded to drink from it. My friend wished me luck and left me alone to the amusement of the bar staff and other customers. I managed a few more rounds in my new drinking container before deciding to leave (without my pandy) to meet and take Edmund with me for a drink in another town, where we would have a choice of several bars.

Later that night, Edmund and I were asked to leave a bar and I genuinely believed it was unwarranted, as we were not misbehaving in any way. I didn't know what I had done to deserve a barring, so I asked Edmund what he had done. His reply was, "I don't know either," so once again, I felt like it was our reputation that had us barred and not our actions. With the lifestyle I was leading back then, due to my alcoholism and reckless character, I just flipped, and true to form, we started smashing up the bar. I later had to pay £500 for the damage caused.

Immediately after that incident, we entered another bar from which I was rightly barred. The barman there kept his cool and continued to serve us while he waited for the Guards to arrive. I'm sure he heard the commotion earlier and was probably expecting our visit. Only one Garda arrived and he asked me to leave, but I told him we would only come with him on the condition that he would drive us to another bar, where I knew we would both get served. He agreed, and as we were travelling in our state sponsored taxi, I remember being in the front passenger seat wearing the Guards hat. Meanwhile, Edmund was sitting in the back and at times he would burst into song and several times, between verses, he told the Guard he had a good mind to thump him and take control of the driving himself. As you can imagine, the landlord in the next bar was not impressed when he saw the patrol car pulling up at his door and Edmund and myself jumping out. The Garda refused our offer of joining us for a drink!

Continuing to Live Life on the Edge

I continued on my binge and during this same period, I met up with Joe, an old mate who I hadn't seen for some time. Joe was driving, so we started off on a pub crawl going from town to town. We were both pretty drunk and Joe suggested that I should be his co-pilot. Over the next few miles everything was going okay and I was keeping him informed of what route we were taking.

We were driving down a road that was straight for about one mile, but which had a fairly sharp corner veering left at the end of it. We were now travelling at a fast speed and as we approached the corner Joe asked, "Which way now co-pilot?" I was certain he knew the route himself, so I just thought I would call his bluff and replied, "Sharp right". I couldn't believe it when Joe followed my instructions and in the next few seconds we both found ourselves crashing through a fence before ending up in an upside-down car, half-way across somebody's field. The car was completely wrecked. Miraculously, we narrowly avoided a telegraph pole and a large iron sign-post which were situated with just enough space for us to pass through. Had we collided with either, I have no doubt our accident would have been fatal.

We were both sore and bruised for a week or so but, thank God, we didn't receive any serious injuries. Needless to say, that was our last rally together.

I remember being involved in two other car accidents, which also could have been fatal. In the first one, my mate Noel and myself had consumed a large amount of drink in various pubs. Noel was driving, and fell asleep. I was so drunk that I didn't realise the danger involved, and casually reached for the steering wheel with my right hand. By that stage, Noel was slumped over with his foot on the throttle. The car was increasing in speed as I tried to steer along the road. We were now approaching a corner at a bridge, with a big drop into a river. I don't even think I knew what road we were on so, as you can imagine, we never managed to take that corner. Instead we found ourselves in mid-air before crashing into a tree, which probably stopped us from ending up in the river. It was the passenger's side of the car that hit the tree.

Noel woke up with the impact of the crash and asked me if I was okay. I was trapped in the car, which was now lying on its side. But I still had my crazy sense of humour and replied, "No I'm dead, so just reverse her out!" Noel put his big hand into my face as he pushed himself up and climbed out the front windscreen, which was shattered.

A neighbour had come on the scene and met Noel as he was climbing back up onto the road. He asked if there was anybody else in the car and Noel said, "No, I'm on my own."

"Well," the neighbour remarked, "it's a good job you were alone, as no passenger would have survived that crash".

Noel completely forgot about me, and it was only when the neighbour took a closer look at the car that he realised I was still in it. At that stage, Noel had got himself a lift to a nearby pub and was busy drowning his sorrows.

The next accident happened in completely different circumstances. I had just come out of a pub at closing time and noticed my neighbour Jimmy getting into his car. I shouted at him and asked him to wait for me as I needed a lift. Either he didn't hear me, or maybe he just didn't want to give me a lift, because he started moving off as I was approaching. I just managed to reach the back door, got it open and scrambled in head first. The car was gathering speed as I was struggling to get my feet in and close the door.

Jimmy, the driver, had also been on a binge and was suffering from the horrors. As we sped up the road I was shouting at Jimmy, telling him to switch on his headlights; Jimmy was too busy talking and swearing to himself. When I realised he was driving up a side road leading into a beach I shouted at him to stop, asking him did he realise where he was going.

Jimmy turned around and said, "I'm going to drown you!"

So when I asked him, "and what about yourself?" he replied, "I'm going to drown myself as well".

I knew then Jimmy had completely lost the plot, and in my panic I reached out, pulled the handbrake, and tried to grab hold of the steering wheel. We were now fighting over the controls, so the next thing I know we are careering up a large sand dune and the car flipped over on its side. Jimmy managed to climb out of the car and as I was laying dazed, with my head on the floor and my feet across the back seat, I hear him shout, "Get out you lazy so and so, and give us a push to see if we can get her back on the road".

By the time I managed to climb out, Jimmy had disappeared, so I set off walking for home. I heard later that Jimmy had gone for help, but could not remember where we had crashed. It was later the following evening when Jimmy eventually found his car.

I had been thinking about going to America for some time as I had always wanted to see it. In order to travel to the States, I had to get myself a passport and visa, and with this in mind I set off for Dublin. This time I brought my nephew Seamus with me as I figured we would only have to stay for one night at the most.

After doing the necessary paperwork at the Irish Embassy office in Ballsbridge, I was told I could collect my documents the following day. I then booked Seamus and myself into the Gate Hotel on Parnell Street in Dublin city centre. Eight days later, Seamus and I were still in Dublin. On the eighth morning, I suggested to Seamus that we should go to London for a drink. Thank God, Seamus talked us out of it, so instead we got the bus back up to Donegal.

During that period, I was fairly familiar with the nightlife and pub scene in Dublin and used to regularly get the bus down to the city. I would book myself into a B&B in the city centre, and hit the town.

I used to enjoy the freedom and the choice of bars and clubs it gave me. My favourite haunts were a club called Rumours, which was next to the Gresham hotel on O'Connell Street, and just down from that was another disco bar called McGraths. Then there was Bojangles on Harcourt Street, Sachs Hotel out in Donnybrook, and the Arlington Hotel on Bachelors Walk. There was also the two O'Sheas, one on Merchant Quay and the other on Talbot Street. There was another club out in Portmarnock that I would have gone to as well.

As well as all of those, I had the wine bars, and last but not least, Barry's Hotel, which I also enjoyed visiting. I knew which nights would be the best to visit each haunt. Thank God I never did get into any bother there. It was a good city if you wanted to drink twenty-four hours a day, which I always did when I was still awake. Looking back, I must have pissed every bed in every B&B in and around Dublin city centre. After my mishap, I always felt very embarrassed, so I tried to make sure I didn't book the same place again. But on several occasions, I discovered a rubber mattress on my bed and figured I must have been there before, having left my trademark.

Going to America

My mate Tommy had emigrated to Philadelphia in 1983 and had done well for himself. We had remained in contact and in the earlier years it was mainly by old-fashioned letter writing. Tommy told me he used to show my letters to his lady friends as they always contained some funny and crazy stories. I remember I used to be laughing myself whilst writing them.

After talking with Tommy on the phone, I made my travel arrangements. I booked a flight from Dublin to JFK Airport in New York, and also booked myself a seat on a coach that would take me to Tommy's house in Philadelphia. I decided I would stay for a total of ten days.

After arriving at Tommy's house, we went for a drink and that same night we ended up at a disco bar. Tommy had to leave early in the morning for his work, and warned me to wait until he returned, and we would both go for a drink.

The following day I awoke around lunchtime and I was craving a drink, and I didn't have the patience to wait for Tommy to return. I decided I would go for a walk and figured that the bar we were in the previous night was within walking distance. The first bar I came upon, I entered. Tommy had introduced me to Coors beer the night before, so I figured a few beers would do me no harm and it would help to pass the time while waiting on Tommy to return.

There was a payphone located inside the bar door, so I decided I would phone home. As I was trying to figure out what coins to use,

I was approached by a lady who asked if I needed help. I handed her the number I wanted to call and after she got me connected, she returned to her seat at the bar.

After my phone call, as I was returning to the bar, I noticed my lady friend waving me over. She was with a girlfriend, so I went over and thanked her for her help. I then bought them both a drink and joined their company.

Everything was going well and a few hours later everything was going even better, as Lisa's girlfriend had now left. I knew I had scored. When Lisa asked if I wanted to go back to her girlfriend's house for a drink, I told her it sounded like a good idea, so Lisa bought a six pack of Coors beer at the bar. But I thought that it wouldn't be enough, so I bought two more six packs for good measure. I was actually tempted to buy a bottle of brandy as well, but I was trying to keep it cool and go with the flow.

Lisa had her car parked outside the bar and didn't seem to be worried about drinking and driving. I was on a great high, laying chilled out in the passenger seat of Lisa's little sports car. We arrived at her girlfriend's house and I was delighted when her friend produced a bottle of whiskey saying, "That damn beer won't be strong enough for an Irishman".

A short time later, the drinks were flowing, the music was playing and the next thing I knew, I was dancing with the two girls – slow dancing, Irish dancing and dirty dancing. I was having a great time, but in the midst of all the action, I had forgotten to phone Tommy and let him know where I was. It was now after 7pm and he probably would have been concerned and wondering where I was. I asked Lisa's friend if I could use her phone. When Tommy answered the phone, he asked where I was. I told him I hadn't a clue, but assumed I was still in America as I hadn't got on a plane or crossed any water. I told him not to worry as I was in really nice company and I would catch up with him later. Tommy gave me the name and address of a bar where I could meet him later.

Lisa then suggested we visit another friend of hers. I was amazed at Lisa's character and stamina, as once again she didn't hesitate in driving her car. We had only travelled a short distance when Lisa asked me if I had ever done coke. I told her I hadn't, and she then said, "Would you mind if I did some?" I told her I didn't mind at all. I hadn't a clue about drugs but I knew she was referring to cocaine.

We stopped outside a house and after hooting the car horn, two men came out and walked over to our car. Lisa told me to join her in the back seat as the two men got into the front seats and one of them took over the driving. Even though I had a quantity of Coors beer and whiskey inside me, I was beginning to feel nervous and on edge. The man in the passenger seat handed Lisa a package and several times he asked the same question as to where she picked me up. I was relieved when we arrived at a bar, as both of the men were now questioning my motives and I knew they were unhappy with my presence.

As we were waiting for our drinks to be served, I told Lisa to excuse me while I went to the toilet. I knew I had to make my escape as I had no doubt I had got myself into a dangerous situation. The bar was very busy which made it easier for me to make my way outside unnoticed. Once outside I got a bad feeling about the street in which I found myself. There was very little traffic and the whole surrounding area had an eerie quietness and darkness about it. I crossed the street and entered a restaurant and asked the waiter how I could order a taxi, telling him I had just arrived from Ireland on holidays and somehow found myself lost and stranded.

He seemed amused at my situation, but was happy to make the call himself. The taxi operator told us it would be forty minutes at least before the next cab would be available. I didn't want to wait that long and I was now becoming very paranoid. I asked the waiter again would he be so kind and make another call for me. This time we rang Tommy's house. His friend answered and told us Tommy had already gone down to the bar, hoping that I might be there. When I told her the name of the street I was in, she confirmed my fears and said, "Martin Jim, you're in a bad neighbourhood".

I was now becoming desperate and I gave the waiter the name and address of the bar that I wished to get to and asked him would it be possible to walk there. He looked at me and said, "You don't want to be walking around here." I told him I was prepared to take my chances. My friend told me it was a twenty minute walk and, after receiving my directions, I started out on my journey. I blessed myself and started praying to St Anthony, asking for his protection and guidance, as I tried to remember as best I could the directions I had been given. Although I was aware I had steered off the intended route, I was afraid to ask again for directions, in case I asked the wrong character. I was walking for almost an hour before I eventually found the street and the bar I was looking for. Tommy was there and when he told me he was glad to see me, I said I sure was glad to see him as well.

I was in a bar in Philadelphia at 7.30am the day I was due to return home. I don't remember leaving it and neither do I remember the bus journey down to New York. I do, however, remember going into JFK Airport. I had four hours to wait until my flight was due to leave. When I was checking myself in, the lady at the desk advised me not to have any more drink. Needless to say, I ignored her and went straight to the bar.

I managed to get through security and while I was waiting to board, I got talking to a lady called Samantha, who was going to Ireland for the first time. Like me, she was travelling alone. We were getting on so well that she got her seat number changed, so that we would be together. We also agreed we would like to spend some time together in Dublin. I was so relieved when we made it onto the plane, as I had been concerned that I had taken too much drink and was completely shattered.

Going to America

I was looking forward to getting some badly needed sleep and to having Samantha's company in Dublin. I was seated on the aisle seat. Samantha was next to me and there was a gentleman at the window seat. I was just talking to Samantha in my usual manner, and I can't remember if I used any swear words during our conversation. If I did, I wouldn't have meant anything by it, and definitely wouldn't have meant to offend anyone. I was surprised then when the gentleman told me to mind my language. I honestly didn't know what he was on about, so I told him to mind his own business as I wasn't talking to him.

We were still on the runway at this stage and he had called for assistance to have me removed. He also said that I had threatened him, which I had not, so I now wanted to clock him. Samantha must have been sorry for changing her seat, as she was now caught in the middle of it all. The stewards approached me and told me I would have to get off the plane. By this stage, the man was really making a scene and was blowing it all out of proportion.

As I reached for my hand luggage, I asked the stewards to ask Samantha what really happened. In the meantime, my mind was racing and I started off telling the stewards how upset I was, because I was on my way home to my mother's funeral. I also added that I was very sorry if I had offended anyone. After a brief talk with Samantha, the stewards took me down to a seat at the back of the plane. Once I got seated and had nobody to talk to, I soon fell into a deep sleep.

I'm not sure how far into our flight we were when I woke up again, so thirsty and dry that my mouth felt like the inside of an old slipper. I could hardly speak, so I signalled to the air hostess. When she came over, I asked her for a drink. She said that if I was lucky I might get a glass of water. After pleading my case, I managed to get a few cans of lager that kept me going until we finally touched down at Shannon airport.

We didn't have much time to spare before our short flight to Dublin, but I was so relieved to be back on Irish soil again that I didn't care if I missed it. I was enjoying a drink at the bar and I could hear my name being called to board. I was undecided on what to do. I knew I had blown my chances with Samantha and I didn't even care about being separated from my luggage. I decided to get back on, and once again I boarded the plane. I was now met by a different air hostess, who was obviously unaware of our earlier incident. She asked me for my boarding card, so when I showed it she directed me to my seat. As it was the same boarding card, I now found myself heading back to the seat I had been removed from.

When my old friend saw me approaching, he put his hands up in the air and screamed, "Keep him away from me, he is a lunatic!" Samantha just buried her face in her hands.

The air hostess rushed down and ushered me into another seat. I was just about seated when another gentleman came down and said, "You're sitting in my seat!" It was just like playing musical chairs, so once again I had to get up. For the remainder of the short flight into Dublin, I remained standing and talked to the air hostesses. They asked me what really happened between myself and the gentleman in New York. I told them that I didn't mean to offend anyone and that I was surprised when he confronted me in the first place. I also added that I felt a bit hard done by when I was moved from seat to seat. They promptly replied that if they had detected the amount of alcohol I had consumed, I would have been refused permission to board in the first place.

Some days later I rang Tommy to thank him for his hospitality, and he said, 'Martin Jim, I didn't realise you had such a serious drink problem', and I answered, 'Neither did I'.

Going to Glasgow

After the New Year in 1992, I once again decided I needed a change of scenery to make a new start for myself. I don't know what possessed me to go to Glasgow, but that was where I landed, with my good intentions.

Although I was aware that Anne, my ex-fiancée was probably still living there, I made the decision that I wouldn't bother contacting her. After staying at my mate Eamonn's house for a few nights, I got myself a large room in a lodging house. The landlord said he was registered and would accept social welfare, so I got myself registered with a doctor, was declared unfit for work and got signed on again at the local social welfare office. I also made a claim for my rent allowance.

I now felt good, having all that sorted. I had £33,000 of my compensation left, so my plan was to find myself a part-time job and ease up on my drinking and get my social life sorted out. The landlord said he kept a good house and would not tolerate any noise or messing about. Well, true to form, once again I started on another serious bender. My landlord could not figure me out at all. He knew I wasn't working.

One day, I was on a pub crawl in Glasgow city centre and while I was making my way down a street, I was approached by a nice lady. She didn't state her occupation, but she said she would give me a blow job for £10. After handing over the agreed price, we moved into an alleyway and she set about her side of the bargain. Everything was going well until she suddenly jumped up and screamed, "Run, the police are coming!"

Now I was in a predicament. The police were coming instead of me and my lady friend had disappeared around a corner with my £10. After I got my trousers pulled up, I ran after her shouting, "Come back with my money, you thief". I ran into the first bar I came to. I was out of breath and was all flustered, so after ordering a drink, I went into use the toilet. You can imagine my shock when I discovered I was still wearing a condom.

Three months later I was still in Glasgow and still on my bender. I was drinking brandy and remember losing my voice for a period, which was frightening. My doctor said it was as a direct result of my alcoholism and strongly advised me to quit drinking. One day, James, another lodger in the house, asked me was I going for a drink. This same character had already received a good few drinks at my expense on a previous occasion, but that didn't bother me, although I was beginning to question his whole character, so I said "Sure, let's go for a wee drink".

I knew there was a hotel located nearby, so I figured it would be as good a place as any to put my mate to the test. After arriving at the counter, I ordered myself a double brandy and a pint for my house mate. I swallowed my drink immediately, and banged my empty glass down on the counter and said, "It's your round now". James was perched up on a high stool, and was just putting his pint up to his mouth for his first sip, and said, "Sorry Paddy, I don't have any money". I said "Well I guess the party's over" and hit him a right hook, knocking him from his seat. James was picking himself up from the floor as I made a speedy exit.

I woke up on the Glasgow to Donegal coach with no recollection whatsoever of getting on it. We were at Stranraer Harbour. I was alone on the coach as everybody else had boarded the ferry. I checked my pockets for money and when I counted enough out, I purchased a ticket and got on board. I figured it would be my quickest way of getting a drink. I had no idea or plan at that moment as to where I was going, but I needed a drink so bad that I would have sailed anywhere to get it.

Once on board, I was like a cat waiting on a mouse for the bar to open. When it finally opened, the ship was shaking and I was shaking and almost collapsed when the barman said, "I can't serve you, as you've had enough already". I was too weak and in too bad a form to plead my case and was now in a bad predicament. Here I was on a ship that I didn't want to be on, with a barman who would not serve me.

I was just about to turn and walk away when a lady, who had been talking with the barman, asked me what I was drinking. I told her that I'd love a brandy and port and was really grateful when I now found myself getting served. The lady was smiling as she walked down to a table with her own drink and sat down alone. I was wondering to myself if she was travelling on her own. Every time I looked down at her table she was smiling and just shaking her head at me. I was waiting for some man to join her. I figured he might have just been at the toilet or something like that.

After some more drinks, I was now beginning to hit form again, and as my mysterious friend was still alone, I decided it was time to buy her a drink and join her at her table. When you meet someone for the first time, you have so much to talk about – a lady said to me one time in London that one night stands can be very exciting, explaining, "You are giving me attention, and I am giving you attention". I suppose it only gets complicated when you fall in love. So after I thanked her for changing the barman's mind, I was then ready to interview her.

I almost fell from my seat when Maureen told me what had happened. The previous night I had met her in a club and she had told me she was going home to Donegal in the morning. I then obviously told her that I needed a wee break myself and would come with her. Apparently, we continued drinking until it was time to get the coach, which departed from the Gorbals area of Glasgow. I must have been on autopilot and once we sat down on the coach, I fell into a comatose sleep. When I finally awoke, my mind was a complete blank. I had no luggage or anything with me, so I decided I would travel on to my home in Carrigart that day. Maureen and I arranged to meet in Letterkenny at 2pm the following day for a drink, but I never made it.

I phoned my landlord some days later and told him I wouldn't be returning. I also contacted the social welfare department and once again cancelled my benefit claims.

Well and Truly Beat

Back at home I continued on my binge. When I wasn't in a pub, I needed a bottle by my side. Even though my money was also coming to an end, I couldn't get motivated to make a claim for disability or unemployment benefit. I was fighting a survival game, and living one day at a time.

One morning, after I went into a bar, the landlady advised me to seek professional help as "You are going to kill yourself drinking." She did serve me two drinks all the same, but said that was all she would give me.

I was completely shattered and a nervous wreck. so I phoned my doctor for an appointment. The doctor had no hesitation in referring me for admission to the psychiatric department at St Conal's Hospital, Letterkenny.

I then took this crazy notion that I might as well have one last good session before signing myself in. Being completely ignorant of my alcoholism, I had assumed that once I presented myself to the hospital, the professionals would do the rest, and cure me immediately. A friend of mine was driving me to the hospital, so I got him to stop off at a bar along the way.

I was so messed up with drink that I remember throwing my referral letter over the counter. The barman gave it back to my friend and that same night I finally arrived at the psychiatric unit in a drunken and pitiful state. Once I was shown my bed I just crashed out.

When I awoke some hours later, I was determined to leave again and had to be sedated to prevent me from going. On waking the following morning, I was so uncomfortable in my new surroundings. I was sharing a room with three other patients who were also going through their own states of distress. I just wanted to be in a room on my own where I could bury my head in my pillow and not have to meet or talk to anyone.

When my doctor came in to talk with me, I told him I wanted to go home. Although he strongly advised me to stay, I signed myself out against his wishes. I remember feeling so weak, it was a struggle trying to sign the form requesting my discharge. Looking back, I probably only went into hospital out of sheer desperation, but I still hadn't addressed my problem.

I only managed to stay off the drink for three weeks after that and it seemed like ages at the time. I went out to a nightclub with the good intentions of not drinking, and I did order and drink a few minerals, but I just wasn't comfortable, so I thought a few drinks would do no harm. I also figured that I would just wait until close to closing time to have my drink and not bother with it during the day. Well, that was wishful thinking. After the first four or five drinks that night, I was feeling so good and so relaxed. I even questioned why I should torture and deprive myself of something that made me feel this way. That is probably the feeling and experience a social drinker can expect at all times, but not me. I was an alcoholic, and once I took my first drink I was back to square one.

The Death of My Father

My father had said to me on several occasions that he would love to see me meet a good woman, stop drinking, and settle down. My father was now eighty years of age and was developing several health problems, but rather than face up to reality, I just tried to put it to the back of my mind.

One night my father fell from his bed, and was unable to move or lift himself up, he had been calling for me to come to his assistance. I was lying in my piss-soaked bed, and was in a comatose state. I never heard his cry for help, and it was another family member who discovered our father when they came to visit the following morning. My mother then suggested Daddy should go up to her home, and stay there while he recovered from pneumonia acquired due to his night lying on the floor.

This should have been a wake-up call for me, as I was aware of his ailing health. I was just too messed up with drink to act responsibly, and take care of the man who I loved so much. After Daddy went to my mother's house, I borrowed £100 from his wallet without telling him. I intended replacing it once I had returned from the bank, but I kept putting it off from day to day. An alcoholic always wants to make sure they have enough money for their next drink.

On the 20th March 1993, my father took a turn for the worse. He was still at my mother's house and the rest of my family were with him. I was drinking in a bar that was about a forty-five-minute drive away, so they sent my mate John to get me. When he arrived at the bar, the Gardaí were already there looking for me, for a different reason.

A fight had started and the barman wanted us removed. We left the bar and nobody got arrested. When I finally got back to my mother's house, my father had already passed away. I was too drunk to notice, and I fell asleep in a spare room.

When I awoke a short time later from my semi-comatose state, my mother broke the sad news to me. I was devastated, and so many memories of all the worry I caused my father raced through my mind. I was craving for a drink so I went off to the pub once again. This time I didn't stay too long in the bar as I wanted to be with my father, whose body had been removed to our own home for his wake. Before I left the bar I ordered a huge carry out of drink, hoping I would have enough to keep me topped up, and hopefully relaxed enough to face the crucial days ahead.

When I returned home with my supply of drink, I set about hiding it at various locations outside our house. I do remember my sister Bridie finding me in our shed, and when she saw some of my supply, she looked at me, and said, "Is it a cure you're looking for, or a bloody party?"

I somehow managed to carry out my responsibilities during the two nights' wake, but I kept myself topped up with my supply of drink. On the morning of the funeral, I was feeling so weak, and since I wanted to help carry my father's coffin, I told both my brothers to make sure they gave me the lighter end of the coffin. The wake and funeral, although a blur in my mind, passed off without incident. It is a regret I will have for the rest of my life that I was not there for my father when he needed me most. I continued on my binge, but no matter how much I drank, I just couldn't get into good form. I was well beyond the stages of getting the 'cure'. I also got arrested again in a public bar for assault but thankfully the landlord didn't look to have me prosecuted in court.

One day, I was alone in my house. It was about six months after my father had died, and I was still on my binge. I remember feeling so messed up and at a very low point in my life. I was in our hallway, and I saw the figure of my father appear in front of me. I just stared at him for some time and I was speechless. It was a strange, but comforting, experience. I remember thinking at that moment, "This can't be for real, and it must be my imagination". Daddy remained there for a short time, and I remember reaching out and trying to touch him.

My first instinct was to phone my mother, but I decided against that as I didn't want to alarm her. Later on I did go up and visit my family, and told them my experience. Although I know that day I was suffering from the horrors, I'm convinced that Daddy did come back to me, to let me know that he was watching over me and to help me get myself sorted.

My mother asked me if I would like to talk with someone. I said I would like to talk to our parish priest, Fr Patsy Gallagher. Fr Patsy was a powerful man, and I knew I could put my trust in him. I spoke to him on the phone, and he said he would be up to see me shortly. I was in a bedroom of my mother's house waiting for him to arrive. I was desperate for a drink, and was so bad with my nerves and paranoia that I climbed out the window.

Once on the roadway, I managed to stop a car and got a lift to a pub. After I got my drink at the bar, I was so bad with the shakes that I was afraid I'd spill it. I took my drink into the toilet and used both my hands to raise it to my mouth, and followed that same procedure several times until I settled a little bit.

I was still in the bar about an hour later, and I decided to phone my mother, and tell her of my whereabouts. She told me she was shamed as she had brought the priest into the room only to discover that I had gone out the window. I apologised to my mother, and I was genuinely sorry for embarrassing and worrying her. Fr Patsy was still in my mother's house, and when he spoke to me I told him where I was. He told me to remain there, as he would come down to see me.

When he came in, we shook hands and I said, "Father, I'm sorry for not waiting on you."

He said, "Martin Jim, I understand. You needed a cure".

We then had a good talk about anything and everything and as he got up to leave, he shook my hand again and said, "Maybe after this you will get eased up on it?"

I continued on drinking for one week after that. During that week, I remember being at home and going through the horrors and imagining the ceilings were bursting with water pouring down and drowning me. I raced into the next room to escape only to experience the exact same thing again. I went up to my mother's house, and we called the doctor. I was sitting on the bed, and I was drenched in sweat. The doctor came in and was holding a jar of tablets in his hand. He asked my brother Edmund to bring us in a glass of water. I was so far gone I thought the doctor wanted the glass of water for himself, so I shouted out to Edmund, "You better bring me in a glass as well".

I'm not sure how many days my tablets were supposed to last, or how strong they were, but I do know that the following morning I was still awake and hadn't slept a wink. I had finished the full course of tablets during the night and was still a bundle of nerves.

That morning I made my way to a hotel where I knew I would get served a drink, it was 7.30am. A few hours later, another old drinking buddy joined me at the bar. At 11am, official opening time, Bertie suggested we walk the short distance to another bar and this time it was Bertie who got refused a drink. Bertie threatened to wreck the joint if he didn't get served. We all knew the threat was serious so I asked my friend to take a seat, and to settle himself. The bar staff were now looking up to me, and seemed very relieved when Bertie took my advice and sat down on the bar stool.

The place was in silence as I turned to Bertie, and said, "You just relax yourself there, and leave the wrecking up to me". I just flipped then and began smashing up the place. I'm not sure how much

The Death of My Father

damage I had caused before I left, but I went into another bar next door and I was served there.

A short time later, Johnny, who had been drinking in the bar I had just smashed up, came in and said, "Do you mind if I join you for a drink?" He went on to explain that he had to leave the other pub because the rain was blowing in the broken windows. The landlord whose pub I was now drinking in informed me that the Gardaí had arrived next door.

"Well," I replied, "Don't worry, I won't have them calling in here looking for me".

I then walked out and straight back into the damaged bar. The landlord and the Gardaí were now assessing the damage, so I just shouted, "Okay boys, let's get out of here". Bertie had disappeared by this stage. I walked out and jumped into the patrol car before the Gardaí came out. Mind you, it's probably a good job that the keys weren't left in the ignition!

For some silly reason, I thought that the Gardaí would just leave me home, but when they went in the opposite direction I asked, "Where are we going now?"

The Garda in the passenger seat turned to me and said, "You're in serious trouble now Martin Jim, and you will be in Mountjoy Prison tonight".

They took me to the station, charged me, and later that same day my case was heard at a special sitting of Castlefin District Court. I had a Garda sitting on each side of me and the drink was dying inside me. I could feel myself going into the horrors once again. One of the Gardaí then asked me if I had much money, as I'd need to employ a good solicitor. I told him I needed all my money for drink and I wanted legal aid. I did get legal aid that day. My case was called and in fairness to the Gardaí and the landlord, they didn't go against me. They were probably thinking that I had enough of a struggle ahead with my severe addiction to alcohol.

I was released on my own bail. My case was adjourned for one month on the condition that I seek professional help and address my alcohol problem. The guards brought me home after my court appearance, but once they had driven off my street, I made my way back down to the village where they had earlier arrested me and continued drinking.

Two days after that I was so bad with the horrors, I was convinced I was going to die. I rang my good friend Fr Patsy and told him that I had continued on drinking since we last talked, but that now I was well and truly beat, and was prepared to go once again into St Conal's Psychiatric Hospital for the professional help I so badly needed. This time I was determined to see it through. I asked Fr Patsy if he'd say a prayer for me.

Fr Patsy said something to me that day I will never forget. He said "Martin Jim, if you go up there now and sign yourself in, you will never look back."

After hearing the reassuring and positive words from my parish priest I rang my brother Eunan and asked him to drive me to the hospital. As I waited for my lift, I went for a short walk up the field behind our house. I remember praying to Daddy and apologising for letting him down in his time of need. I also asked him and St Anthony to watch over and help me with my struggle ahead. I remember thinking and saying to myself, "If I do get myself out of this mess, it will be a long time before it happens again." I also cried my eyes out on that lonely walk.

APPENDIX TO BOOK ONE

Some Solicitors' Letters

As a matter of reference, and for the reader's interest, I have inserted four solicitor's letters below, relating to some of the incidents I was involved in. It is interesting that not one of these letters has my correct home address.

Mr. Martin McFadden,
Dunmore, Carrigart,
via Letterkenny,
Co Donegal.   14th November, 1984

Dear Sir,

We act for Mr. . . . the Proprietor of . . . and the . . .

The purpose of this letter is to inform you that you are hereby barred from admission to any of these premises and also to inform you that a claim will be made against you for the damage which you caused to our client's property, as soon as the extent of the damage has been ascertained.

Yours faithfully,

* * * * * * * *

Mr Martin McFadden,
Carnagore,
Carrigart   15th April, 1988

Re: DISTRICT COURT

Dear Martin,

As you are aware, at the District Court in . . . your were fined a sum of £4.00 for drunk and disorderly and £4.00 for disorderly behaviour.

In relation to the assault on . . . Charge, you were given a one month's suspended sentence and you were fined £50 in relation to damage and given three months to pay the fine.

We would point out to you that the District Justice was extremely annoyed with you . . . as regards this incident in . . . and he was inclined to send ... you to jail. However, while I feel things worked out O.K. in the District Court this time, I would certainly feel that if you get into any further problems with the Gardai or other people in the foreseeable future, that the District Justice is going to take a very poor view of matters and will probably send you for a jail sentence. We must therefore advise you strongly to keep on the right side of the law and the Gardai for the foreseeable future so that these matters would not in any way affect the running of your personal accident claim.

Our fee and expenses in relation to attending at the District Court in ... amount to the sum of £70.00 and again, we would suggest that as you are not in receipt of much at present that this fee would not be paid until your entire claim is finalised.

* * * * * * * *

Messrs Martin & Edward McFadden,
Dromore, Carrigart,
Co Donegal.   23rd December, 1991

Re:– ...

Dear Sirs,

We have been instructed by our client ... to write to you with regard to an incident which occured on Monday the 23rd inst. when you entered into our clients premises and caused severe damage, destruction, nuisance and annoyance therein.

Please note that it is our understanding that the damage caused by both of you is in excess of £500.00 and our client of the ... instructs us that if we do not hear from you stating that you will compensate her in full for damage, expenses, outlays and legal costs we are instructed to issue proceedings against you.

We also have instructions to bar you from entering the ... in future or else we will be forced to initiate injunction proceedings against you.

Please let us hear from you within 14 days admitting liability and stating that you undertake not to enter the premises again and to compensate our client for all damage done.

Yours faithfully,

Appendix – Book One

Mr. Martin McFadden,
Dunmore,
Carrigart,
Letterkenny,
Co Donegal.   12th August, 1993

Re: Incident Two Weeks ago at Licensed Premises Known as . . . in which Garda . . . had to be summoned for Assault on . . .
<u>Our Client:</u> . . .

Dear Sir,

We have received instructions from our above client of the . . . to write to you concerning your behaviour on the above licensed premises on the above date when you were drunk, violent and quarrelsome and disorderly on the date in question.

This is to inform you that from the date hereof you will be refused admittance to the above licensed premises at all times for any purpose until such further notice and if you attempt to gain entry and disregard this Notice, the Licensee will not hesitate to contact the Gardai and issue proceedings against you without further notice.

                           Yours faithfully.

BOOK TWO

My Recovery

That same evening, I arrived once again at the admissions office of St Conal's Psychiatric Hospital in Letterkenny. It was the 29th September, 1993. I was thirty years of age; I had only £4,000 left out of the £90,000 compensation I had received. Although I could account for about £22,000, I had managed to blow £64,000 inside three and a half years.

As I was signing the form for my admission, I begged the doctors to lock me up in a room on my own. I was so frightened of the other patients and so paranoid, I feared for my life and my safety.

After being assessed, I was taken to my bed in an open ward. I remember punching another patient, whom I imagined was coming to attack me. The kind gentleman had only been coming to wish me luck.

I can't remember what medication I received, but I went to hell and back over the next few nights and days. Every single thought that came into my mind created huge worry and stress. I was so depressed and felt desperately alone. I was very frightened of the future, and wished I could go into a deep sleep until my nightmare would be all over.

Whenever I went to the bathroom, I was accompanied by a male nurse. I suppose I had to be under constant observation in case I tried to self-harm or possibly attempt suicide. I found it impossible to get a good night's sleep, perhaps because I was in a six-bedded ward amongst other patients who were also going through their own different states of mind. Maybe that is also part of the therapy, as it was definitely a reality check. It's hard to imagine the mentality of an alcoholic who will drink themselves into such a sad and dangerous state. I only know what I went through myself and I can only imagine the hurt and worry I caused my loved ones.

After spending one week in the hospital, where I received excellent professional care, the doctor agreed I was well enough to be discharged. I had personally apologised to the poor patient I had earlier thumped, and as I was leaving my ward, my heart went out to the other patients who I was leaving behind. I was hoping they hadn't noticed the tears welling up in my eyes. An addiction counsellor had visited me in hospital and I had agreed to start group therapy immediately on my discharge.

The course was for a period of six weeks, Monday – Friday, and was in another part of St Conal's Hospital Campus. There were several counsellors employed there, both male and female. I was lucky that I could get a return lift each day with a friend, which meant I could continue living at home. I know I wouldn't have got through that dark period if I had to live any place other than in the safety of my own home during that time. I needed the love and support of my family.

Although my nerves and paranoia were improving daily, I was still very restless within myself and could become very agitated and aggressive. I was also fairly weak and unsteady on my feet. My father's death was still eating away at me. My counsellor didn't have great hope for me at first; he was suspicious that I might have been just using the course to save me from a possible jail sentence. One day he asked me what I hoped to achieve. I told him I wanted to get sober, get out of trouble, get myself a car and a job, and if I met the right woman I would like to get married and settle down.

I still had my pending court case to answer to. Regardless of its outcome, I was determined to beat the bottle and get my life sorted out. The group therapy course was the next stepping stone on my road to recovery, and I suppose the group was a good distraction for me at the start of my recovery. As well as what I would have been getting out of it, it kept my mind busy and occupied.

I remember several times while walking down the town to get my lift, I would automatically just walk into a bar, through pure force of habit. Sometimes I would turn and walk out and other times I would stay and have a mineral. My counsellors strongly advised me to stay clear of bars in the early stages of my recovery, but it was advice I didn't obey. They also told me I would have to change my whole circle of friends. I had made some good friends while I was drinking, so rather than shut them out of my life completely, I decided I just had to change where and under what circumstances I met up with them.

One morning before my course, I met up with an old friend who had just returned from holidays, didn't realise my situation and gave me a bottle of whiskey as a present. I didn't bother trying to explain and accepted their kind gift, and as I made my way into my course, I tried to think where I could hide my bottle. Although I had no intention of drinking it, I still didn't want to dump it. I figured it would be a nice present for someone who wasn't an alcoholic. I hid my bottle in a bin outside the building, and gave it to a friend at a later date. I told my counsellor about it later and, needless to say, she wasn't impressed.

On another day in our group, my counsellor suddenly asked me to throw my chair through the window. I refused. She then asked, "Why not? Sure that's what you did in the public house".

"Well," I replied, "that was different, because I was drunk that day".

She said, "So it was okay for you to do it because you were drunk. How do you know you won't be drunk tonight?"

So I made a deal with her. I said, "I'll tell you what we will do. Give me a bottle of whiskey now and the choice of drinking it or throwing the chair".

She replied, "And what will you do?"

I answered, "I'll fire the chair!"

She then asked, "And what will we do with the bottle?"

My Recovery

I replied, "As we are all alcoholics in this room, we might as well give the bottle to whoever fixes the window".

As I was waiting for her response, I was looking at a window. We were on the second floor, and if she had put me to the test, I would have had no hesitation in letting fly. Another morning, our counsellor wrote on his blackboard: "I can't means I won't." He went on to explain that, if he asked me to go to the shop, and I said "I can't," it was just the same as saying "I won't". He continued, "You could if you wanted to". Well, I argued that it was not always the same. I added, "If you were to give me a difficult sum to do now, I wouldn't be able to do it; but if I could, I would, but I can't." We all had a laugh at that.

My court case came up again. This time, my counsellor went up with me and spoke very well on my behalf. My case was then put back to be heard in three months' time. After my six-week course of therapy was completed, I then signed a contract undertaking to attend 'after care' for a period of one year. It was only one day per week. Being honest about that, it was a commitment I wouldn't have undertaken except for my pending court appearance. I had to go with the flow, but I had a strong belief I was going to win this battle owing to the power of prayer and my strong faith.

I had now signed on and qualified for unemployment benefit. I also applied for my Provisional Drivers Licence. I then bought my first car, a Ford Fiesta, which cost me £400 – it was all I could afford. The previous owner had replaced its door and its bonnet, and they were now in a different colour to the original. My brother Eunan was a mechanic, and he assured me it was in good working order. so that was all that mattered to me. Although I owned a few motorbikes when I was younger, and drove the family tractor occasionally, I didn't have any experience driving a car. When I was younger I had no interest in owning my own car or learning how to drive, but now I realised I needed one and it was another stepping stone in getting my life together.

After some time driving about locally on my provisional license, I knew that my next move was to get my full licence. After taking my first driving lesson I thought to myself, "I'll never remember half of this," but I knew I had to keep at it if I was going to succeed. I used the driving instructor's car each time for my lessons and took eleven lessons in total. My instructor advised me to apply for my test, as he was confident I would pass.

On the day of the actual test I used the instructor's car for doing my test, as I was now more familiar and confident driving it. I was also praying the Nine Tuesday novena to my friend St Anthony, and once again he answered my call. I passed my driving test on my first attempt. I had such a great feeling of relief that it almost sounded too good to be true. My own car and my full driver's license gave me so much more independence.

My lifestyle and quality of life was improving every day. My counsellors strongly recommended that I should go to AA, but for some reason that never appealed to me. I had my mind made up to get and remain sober and I was fairly confident of achieving it.

My faith and my confidence were increasing every day, but I knew I had to be patient as getting my life sorted was going to be a slow process. My education began and ended at national school level and I didn't have any job qualifications. In addition, my injuries meant I wouldn't be fit for rough oul' work.

I was blessed to have a good home and family and that was a huge benefit to my circumstances. My own car was now an added bonus. I wasn't anxious about earning or having big money about me again – all I wanted was enough money to get me by. Staying sober and out of trouble was my main priority. I still had my court case to answer and I was anxious to get that over with, as it was playing on my mind. I couldn't really make any big plans until I knew the outcome of that.

My Recovery

In the meantime I knew the time had come for me to make an appointment with the dentist and have some important work done to my teeth, which I had neglected for years. My dentist suggested he would fit a bridge to replace the denture plate (front teeth) I had been wearing from my teenage years. After several visits to my dentist I was very pleased with the outcome.

I stopped counting the number of times I lost my dentures due to vomiting bouts brought on by my excessive drinking. It was a horrible, depressing feeling to wake up and immediately realise that your denture plate was gone, with no recollection whatsoever about where it might have occurred. It would mean having to make an appointment with a dentist and go through the same procedure of having impressions taken before receiving the new denture. It was costly and embarrassing and I would try to avoid meeting people while I was waiting for the new teeth.

As well as being alcoholic, I also have an addictive personality – almost everything has to be to excess. One time when I was suffering severe back pain, I got painkillers from a few different sources and in one day I took a total of sixteen. It could have proved fatal, but I was in such agony or horrors at those times that I would look for an immediate cure. Even when doing something as simple as making a hot lemon drink for a cold, I would not be happy with just one sachet, so I would put two or maybe three in at one time.

I now knew the time had come for me to address my diet and exercise routine. I was at least four stone overweight. I would go on eating binges, and still do, but now I'm trying to control it. Once I decided to lose weight that first time, I went on a strict diet and exercise regime. We alcoholics want everything done yesterday and once we set our minds on something it's all systems go.

I didn't get any advice on my new diet but I was quite confident that I would succeed. In the morning, or whenever I would get out of bed (I wasn't working), I would have a cup of tea and two slices of toast with butter. During the rest of the day I would drink cups of water to keep the hunger at bay. For my second and final meal of the day I would have a potato and small piece of meat or whatever was going, I would have this meal before six o'clock each evening. I never worried about getting my five pieces of fruit, veg or whatever, and never bothered with juices or breakfast cereals or any of those fancy things.

I went for walks during that period four and five different times a day. I was completely obsessed with losing weight, and I was too hungry to sit down and relax anyway. Walking was the best exercise for me due to my injuries and it's also really good for both mind and body. I remembered reading an article that if you get up from the table feeling full you will put on weight; if you get up from the table feeling just right, you will maintain weight, and if you leave the table feeling hungry, you will lose weight, so it's really as simple as that.

One time I asked a mate how he kept so fit. He told me that if he ate every time that he was hungry, then he would be a big man. Although I am still slightly overweight, I am happy enough with my figure as I have no desire to possess a six pack. I suppose my eating plan and diet is still very extreme, but it works for me. On a Friday my eating binge begins for the weekend, and I might sit at the TV and stuff myself with every kind of rubbish that I can get my hands on. I am sometimes so full afterwards that I can hardly walk the short distance into my bedroom. I do exactly the same thing on a Saturday, and then I try to cut down on the Sunday, and get back on track for the week ahead. I don't mind going a few kilos over my weight as I know I can take that off in a short space of time.

People have said to me to eat a little every night instead of what I'm at, but it's my addictive personality and I never was happy doing things in moderation. It was the same with my alcoholism and I just couldn't settle for a few drinks. I suppose my binge eating compensates for having to be sober in a strange way.

My Recovery

When my court case came up again, my addiction counsellor and my solicitor both spoke well on my behalf. I had already paid for the damage I had done to the public house and, in fairness to the publican, he didn't go up and give evidence against me. He was happy as long as I could guarantee him that I would steer clear of his pub in the future.

I received a three-month suspended sentence and community work, and felt so relieved it was finally over and dealt with. That day, as I walked out of that courthouse, I swore to myself that it would be a long time before I would be in trouble again.

My community work order involved working at our local football grounds and was for a period of thirty days. The work involved repairing holes in the football pitch and the surrounding area. The football grounds where we were working was situated close to a beach, and since it was all sand, it was ideal for playing football and would have remained dry even during wet weather. Our supervisor was a real gentleman, which certainly made my task much easier and quite enjoyable.

There were two other men with me who had also received a working order penalty for whatever wrongdoing they were convicted. We had some great laughs while we worked off our penalty. Our supervisor was driving a Granada car, so rather than wheeling our barrows we decided we would try and make it as easy as possible. We would place the shafts of the wheelbarrow into the open boot and one of us would sit inside holding them while the driver would tow our load around the football field. As the car was huge, I'm pretty certain we would have been burning a lot of fuel.

A local contractor had a JCB digger machine parked outside his house but both of the back wheels were deflated. We approached him and he agreed we could borrow it on the condition that we would get the punctures fixed. We spent a full day carrying out our side of the bargain. Even though the pitch and surrounding area was pretty level, my work colleagues and I somehow managed to tumble our JCB into a huge hole we had created.

Eventually I got my hours worked off so that was another great weight lifted from my shoulders. Mentally and physically my health was improving every day.

On St Patrick's Day I decided I would go to Buncrana, a town about one hour's drive from my home, where I knew there were some old friends home from London. I took my nephew Seamus with me. I was now less than six months sober and driving down to Buncrana that day I had no intention of drinking or craving for a drink. I met up with some old drinking pals and everything was going good. As we moved about from pub to pub my mind started toying with the idea that maybe I would have a few drinks. I was thinking that myself and Seamus could stay overnight in Buncrana or maybe Seamus could drive my car home.

After a few moments of crazy thinking about 'will I, wont I?' I decided I was going to have a pint. I was now craving for it big time. I turned to Seamus and told him of my plan, Seamus looked at me and I could see the sadness and disappointment in his eyes, he said to me, "Maybe you shouldn't bother". Seamus was wise and cool enough to tell me how much I had achieved since I got sober and how much I had to lose. Looking at Seamus that day and seeing how much he loved me and wanted me to remain sober was enough for me to change my mind. After I got over that bad moment, I was so relieved and grateful to Seamus. Had he not been with me that day I would have drank for certain.

Meeting Liz

One night, I made my way to a nightclub about forty-five minutes' drive from my home. I was enjoying my new-found sobriety and the freedom and independence of having my own car. I had been in this same club the previous Saturday and had been talking to a lady, and we arranged to meet again, so I was now looking forward to my date. My friend still hadn't appeared by 1.15am so I figured I had been stood up.

Time was running out so I decided to take a walk about the dance floor and maybe meet someone else. As I was walking down the floor, a girl approached me and asked would I dance with her friend Liz? After looking at the lady in question, I very quickly realised she was gorgeous, and said I sure would.

I was assuming Liz was in on the plan, so I approached her and, full of confidence, I asked would she like to dance. I was left speechless when she refused, and I thought to myself, "This is some craic, my night is not going so good now".

As I turned to walk away, Liz then grabbed my hand and said, "Oh, maybe I will."

I was thinking to myself, "I wish you would make your mind up."

As we were making our way onto the dance floor, I remember the band was starting into the classic 'Suspicious Minds' song by Elvis Presley. Liz told me she was from Strabane, Co Tyrone, which is part of Northern Ireland.

Later that night, I was surprised when Liz asked what I was doing last year on 29th September. I very honestly told her that was the day

I went into the hospital for detox and I went on to explain all about my alcoholism and crazy living. I was now nine months sober.

It so happened that 29th September was Liz's birthday and that was her reason for asking me the question. Coincidentally, 29th September is also the feast day of Saints Michael, Gabriel, Raphael, our Archangels, so it seems like they played a big part in bringing us together.

Liz also told her friend that first night that she had just met the man whom she was going to marry. Meeting Liz was the best thing that ever happened to me. It transpired that Liz was a pioneer and had never tasted an alcoholic drink. It also proved that, once I had made that decision to quit drinking, my life was improving day by day.

The following Saturday I went with Liz to her friend's wedding. Liz being a pioneer had a huge input into my sobriety. It meant we now didn't have to go to pubs or clubs to socialise. I found that going to the cinema or out for a meal could be very enjoyable. This was a whole new social scene for me. We were also just as happy to stay at home and watch the TV. I suppose the most important thing was we were happy to just be together. Christmas was really enjoyable, and it was my second Christmas to be sober.

In the New Year, I decided it was time for me to seriously start looking for a job. Liz had seen an advert for vacancies for a company called Seagate, an American-based company who had established two factories in Co Derry, Northern Ireland. They specialised in making computer parts and said appropriate training would be provided to the successful applicants.

The vacancy I applied for was in their factory in the Springtown Industrial Estate, just a short distance inside the Donegal border, which would mean a travelling time of one hour each way. The wages were to be paid in sterling, which would add to its value.

When I was filling in the application form I figured I had better

Meeting Liz

tell some lies, and boost my CV, or I wouldn't have a hope in hell of getting an interview. I put down the hotel that I had worked in (and also got sacked from) as a reference, figuring it was such a long time ago that they wouldn't bother contacting them.

Another hotel in which I drank a lot, and where I had a good relationship with the manager, said they would give me a reference if required (It was one of the few places I wasn't barred from). For good measure, I also put in that I had attended Milford Tech (secondary school) for three years.

I was excited and nervous when I got called for my interview. Liz had bought me a shirt, tie and trousers for the occasion. Looking back now, that was my first job interview. When the gentleman interviewing me told me he had also attended Milford Tech, I thought I was in trouble. We looked around the same age, and I thought to myself, "Just my luck, I'm goosed now!"

He asked about three different fellows, who I hadn't a clue about. Without much hesitation I said, "It's a long time since I saw any of them". I then continued my bluffing and said, "last I heard, one was going to Australia, one was talking about going to London and the third fellow was supposed to be getting married."

I was surprised and delighted some time later when I got my letter saying I had been successful. After my first day at work, the excitement had soon gone and reality kicked in big time. I was told my hours were 6am to 6pm on a three- and four-day rota. After one month that would change to a night shift, 6pm to 6am, and rotate accordingly. What really put me off was the strict dress code; I was going to be kitted out in a bodysuit and gloves, and also have to wear a head and face mask, similar to those an astronaut would wear on his way to the moon. It was going to be so claustrophobic, and every second of my time had to be accounted for.

I told Liz that first night that I didn't think I was going to stick it. In fairness to Liz, she told me to do what I thought best and it wouldn't be the end of the road. The next morning I reported for work again, but had already made my mind up. I thought to myself, 'I came through enough of hell during my years of drinking, and I don't want to go through anymore." I walked out of Seagate that evening and never returned.

Although I had no other job prospects or any money, I was so relieved once I made that decision to quit, and I knew it was the right decision. If you are happy in your job you are eager and willing to learn and face any new task that might arise, but having to work somewhere you didn't want to be is a completely different scenario.

I remember reading one time that since there are twenty-four hours in a day, you have eight hours for working, eight hours for leisure, and eight hours for sleep. I suppose that would be in an ideal world.

Shortly after that, I applied for a job in the UNIFI Factory in Letterkenny. As I did at Seagate, I lied on my application form. I got called for my interview and thought it had gone quite well, but this time I wasn't so lucky. I was disappointed and surprised when I got my rejection letter in the post. One good lesson I learned from that interview was in future to copy any more job application forms, etc. that I filled in and keep them as a reminder of what I had actually written.

Starting Work in Letterkenny General Hospital

My next job application was for portering duties in Letterkenny General Hospital. It was advertised in our local paper, and this time I really wanted the job. It was the one place I always thought I would like to work. Despite my last two interview experiences, I still decided I would take another chance and exaggerate my CV. Once again I lied on the application form, but this time I kept a copy. I stated that I had attended secondary school for a three-year period and also stated that I had previously worked as a hotel porter, figuring it would improve my chances. I assumed they wouldn't look for a reference from there as it had been over fifteen years since I had been sacked.

On the day of my interview, I was pleased as I thought it had been very satisfactory. Once again, I was praying hard to my friend St Anthony. When I got my letter informing me that I had been successful, I was so happy.

Sometime after I had started working at the hospital, I met Niall, who had worked with me in the hotel; in fact, he was on duty with me the same day I got sacked. He says to me, "You are one lucky man".

Niall went on to explain that the hospital did, in fact, phone the hotel looking for my reference. The young girl on reception who took the call didn't know me, but Niall was still working there, and just happened to be in the office at that particular moment. The girl then asked my friend if he remembered me. "Yeah," he says, "I sure do." He took hold of the phone and gave the lady from the personnel department of Letterkenny General Hospital a glowing reference on my behalf. It was the break I needed.

My new job was going very well, and in the beginning I worked twelve-hour shifts, six days per week. As well as portering duties, I also got extra shifts working for the domestic and catering departments. My job descriptions certainly varied from day to day. I remember joking to my supervisor one morning that I didn't know whether I should dress in my own clothes or a woman's clothes, as you just never knew what department you could get sent to.

During the summer months, I had the habit of climbing onto the flat roof of a building at the rear of the hospital during my lunch breaks. I would borrow a blanket from one of the wards and, after removing my shirt, I would stretch myself out. One particular day while I was on my sun bed, I fell into a deep sleep, and when I finally awoke I realised I was an hour late for my work. I hurried down from the roof top, but met my supervisor before I got a chance to throw some cold water on my face and think of some good excuse. Needless to say that was the end of my sunbathing on my lunch breaks.

Every twelve weeks you got a 'break of service' for one week, which was the rule while you were temporary. You could sign on the dole for that period and we used to all enjoy that break. When I received the news that they were making my contract a permanent position I was overjoyed. It was a huge relief to now have that little bit of added security regarding my job.

As I was now receiving a regular income, I started to get back on my feet financially, so to speak. I managed to pay off my Credit Union loan and paid for a TV and video that I had taken out on the hire purchase scheme. I was also able to buy new clothes on a regular basis, and Liz and myself went on our first holiday. We also went to my first concert, which was Tina Turner performing live in Dublin.

Starting Work in Letterkenny General Hospital

My life was improving all the time and I was really enjoying my sobriety. During that period I can't remember having any urges to drink, apart from that time in Buncrana. I was now enjoying a lifestyle that I didn't know existed when I was drinking. I was away from the lonely old bar rooms, and all the trouble, paranoia, and depression that went with it. Even though several people suggested I would benefit from attending AA, I was happy and confident enough to continue putting my trust in the power of prayer and my faith in St Anthony.

Christmas was another very enjoyable occasion and it was my third one sober. It meant so much to my mother and the rest of my family. Instead of worrying about me, they could now enjoy the fact that I was now there to share all the happiness and peace that my sobriety had brought us. Although it hurt when I thought of my father's final years and his sad passing, I did get some comfort in the belief that he was still very close and was watching over and protecting me.

During his lifetime, my father had joined a hire purchase scheme and, over quite a number of years, managed to buy our home from Donegal County Council, which was responsible for building it. Daddy had bequeathed our home to me in his will, so I now took great pride in it and got great satisfaction from keeping it maintained to the best of my ability. It was certainly some turnaround from my drinking days, when I was so messed up and insecure and often worried about who would take care of things if my parents were no longer with us.

Since getting sober, I was becoming more confident and capable of standing on my own two feet. I was now enjoying the responsibility of paying the bills, maintaining the house and doing the shopping – chores of everyday life. While I was drinking I wouldn't have been able to do such simple things. I was now living in reality and loving every moment of it.

Liz had been talking for some time about wanting to buy a house in her home town of Strabane, Northern Ireland. My home place in Carrigart was one hour's drive for Liz to get to work, and that was providing the weather was good and the roads okay. It could be a nerve-wrecking journey when there was snow or ice on the roads. Having our own house in Strabane would be ideal for Liz; she would be close to her work and also her family and friends. My journey time of a half-hour drive would remain roughly the same.

After viewing a few different houses, Liz said she had her heart set on one, so once we had secured the required mortgage, we became the new owners. Liz must have been really excited. I suppose I was too, but deep down in my heart I knew I would have a struggle settling there. Although most people would have thought it was our dream home, I knew I wouldn't want to be away from the home where my heart was. It certainly was a big commitment and a huge change of direction in my life. A few short years earlier, I could never have imagined myself in this position. Yes, I had dreamed of getting sober, but I would always have imagined Carrigart as being my permanent home.

Mammy's Stroke and Eventual Death

I was at my work when I received a phone call informing me that Mammy had suffered a severe stroke, and was now on her way into hospital. I made my way to the casualty entrance to meet the ambulance, and I watched in silence as the paramedics removed my mother by stretcher. I knew that, although she couldn't speak or move, she was still aware of my presence. The kind and thoughtful ambulance driver told me to take her hand. As I reached out and held her hand, Mammy gave me a little smile to let me know she was glad to see me.

We walked in silence as we made our way to the medical ward for her admission. My eyes were filled with tears as I was thinking back on all the years she had worked so hard and devoted her whole life for each and every one of us. I was also thinking about and sorry for all the worry and trouble I had put my parents through while I was drinking.

Mammy was eventually transferred to a district hospital as she needed professional care on a twenty-four hour basis, which we as a family couldn't provide for her at home. The district hospital to which she was transferred was close to our new home in Strabane, which made it easier for me to visit. Although I had no desire to drink during that time, I was becoming very unsettled again. I knew deep in my heart that I wouldn't be staying in Strabane long term, but I didn't want to rock the boat while Mammy was ill. When someone you love is ill, you are also sort of ill, and not in good form, as you are worrying and feeling so sorry for them. After a long battle, Mammy passed away on Thursday 8th October 1998. Love you Mammy, may you rest in peace.

The home is never the same again once you lose your parents. I was grateful to God and St Anthony for being sober for the last few years of Mammy's life. I was thinking back to when I was young and all the neighbours and visitors that used to visit our mother's home. Those visits would have been known as raking. One old character used to sit on a chair close to the fire, and he had this habit of leaning back on the chair and sort of rocking to and fro. He also talked loudly to himself.

One night, Mammy asked, Paddy, "Why do you always speak to yourself?", and his answer was simply, "Well it's like this Sadie, you see I like talking to an intelligent man". Mammy also had a great sense of humour so she then said, "Paddy, now don't you be talking while I'm interrupting."

Going Home Alone

I made up my mind that I had to leave Strabane. I was so unsettled, and my head was all over the place. Although I had everything and more that I could ever hope for in Liz, part of me was missing the wild side of life again. I was also missing my old home place in Carrigart too much. My father had so much pride in our home; I knew he would not want me living anywhere else. My little home in Carrigart wouldn't have been as fancy or as well-finished as our new home, but it was where my heart was and where I wanted to be. I wasn't looking forward to breaking the news to Liz, and when I did, Liz wasn't long in coming up with an arrangement that might suit both of us. Liz told me to go on home to Carrigart alone, and she would remain in Strabane.

I was back home alone, and one day, while I was driving past a local pub, I noticed my mate Charlie's car parked outside. On the spur of a second I swerved around in the middle of the road, and drove up to the pub door. It was lucky there wasn't any other traffic on the road, as I didn't even take the time to indicate or check my mirrors. Before I knew it, I found myself up at the bar ordering a pint. It just hit me all of a sudden, and I don't know what came over me. By pure chance, I ordered a pint of Guinness, and as I was waiting for my pint to be served, I went over and joined Charlie at his table.

All sorts of crazy thoughts were racing through my mind just then. I knew I was doing the wrong thing and I was feeling both nervous and excited. Although it was six years since I last drank, I now wanted a drink big time. I was still waiting on my pint to be served, and I thought to myself, "What is keeping him?"

I then looked back up at the bar counter and noticed our barman had disappeared. I got up from my table and went over to investigate. I saw him hiding behind a door, and he seemed to be dialling a number from his phone. I tiptoed over and listened and I heard him talking to his boss on the phone, and this is part of what he said, "What the hell am I going to do? Martin Jim has just come in and ordered a pint". That split second was enough time for me to change my mind as I realised the trouble my drinking again would surely bring about.

I went back over to Charlie's table and said goodbye, and good luck, and walked outside. Had I ordered any other drink apart from Guinness, I would have remained at the bar, thus making it harder for the barman to refuse. I still don't know if he had my good intentions at heart that day, or if it was for his own safety and that of his bar. Had I drank that day, there was a good chance I would have caused trouble, as my head was pretty messed up. Thank God I did not. It just proved that no matter how long I had been sober, I was still very vulnerable.

Edmund had got himself a nice mobile home, and he placed it at the rear of my garden. Living so close to each other meant we saw each other on a daily basis. It was good, and when Edmund wasn't on a binge, I would love going into him for the craic. As a young man, Edmund had worked as a chef for a total of thirteen years in a top class hotel, so it wasn't a problem for him to serve up a tasty dish. At about 2am one morning my phone rang. I answered it and I was still half asleep.

Edmund was on the other end of the line, and he said, "Hello brother, I'm just giving you a wee call to let you know I got myself a new mobile."

I asked, "What is wrong with the mobile you already are living in?"

Edmund then says, "It's a new mobile phone I got, you stupid wee eejit." I laughed and then I told him he should have kept his valuable piece of information until the morning.

Liz Joins Me in Carrigart

Liz came out to Carrigart to meet me. We had been talking several times on the phone prior to that, and we decided we would give our relationship another try. Liz added that we should sell our house in Strabane, and she would be happy to make Carrigart our permanent home. We also made plans and set a date for our wedding.

We went to Alcudia, Majorca for a short break. The weather was really hot, and although I love the sun I can't say I really enjoyed that holiday. I found it very difficult to lie sunbathing for any length of time, because I would get restless and would have to get up and start walking about. Although I love walking, I find that you can only walk so far in the scorching heat, and it was also making me very thirsty. The thought of swallowing a nice big cool pint did cross my mind occasionally.

Liz, on the other hand, could really chill out and she had no problem lying on her sun lounger reading a book. She might not have been so relaxed had she known how thirsty I was becoming as I pranced about with my tongue hanging out.

While we were in Alcudia I bought a beautiful pocket watch for my brother Edmund. One night, I was sitting on a bench by the seaside; I was alone and I was deep in thought. I decided I would write my brother Edmund a postcard, wondering would it be the first mail to arrive at his new address. I can't remember exactly what I wrote, but I do remember laughing to myself as I was writing.

Some days later, Edmund was at home waiting on the postman,

which was a real coincidence. This day in particular Edmund was anxiously awaiting his tractor insurance policy in the post. When the postman arrived at his door, Edmund was certain his valuable package had arrived. When he then discovered it was my stupid postcard, he was so disappointed and annoyed that he raced into our brother Eunan's house with my card and said, "Look at what that stupid wee eejit sent me!"

I went to Galway with a group of my mates for my stag night. I decided it might be a safer option to go outside of my own area with my party and thankfully it all went well. I suppose I was afraid of us getting into trouble if we stayed at home and went out locally. We would have been limited to just a few pubs as there would have been quite a few characters present, including myself. Although I was sober and out of trouble, I still did not feel comfortable socialising in the local bars. I suppose I still had a chip on my shoulder.

One night, Liz and myself went out with some friends to a local bar. The bar we were in had changed management and that was probably the reason we went there. I remember ordering a drink for my company from a young barman whom I didn't know. One of the drinks I had ordered was a pint of Guinness. While I was standing at the bar waiting to be served and was minding my own business, the landlord, whom I had never met before, came over and asked was I okay. I answered yes, I was fine and told him I was just waiting on my pint of Guinness to be served.

He then looked at me straight in the eye and said, "There are two things in here you don't rush, one is the pint of Guinness and the other is me". Then he walked away and went on to serve another customer. Well, I could feel my blood boiling, so after getting his attention again I called him over, and said, "I just want to let you know there are also two things in here that I don't give a damn about, one is the pint of Guinness and the other is you".

Liz Joins Me in Carrigart

During this outburst the young barman appeared with my pint. The landlord walked away and I made my way back to my table. I didn't make anyone in my company aware of what had happened, but as the night went on, I was getting more annoyed thinking about it. I was trying to figure out in my mind why he had said it and was wondering was it because of my reputation when I was drinking, and the fact that I would have smashed that same bar up on several previous owners. In any case, I thought he was out of order and I couldn't settle myself any longer.

As the band were belting out 'I Want to Break Free', I stood up, and after stepping up onto my own stool, I managed to jump and land on top of our table. I could feel the adrenalin rushing through my blood. Liz and the rest of my company were shouting for me to get down, but I took off across the whole bar jumping from one table to the next. I didn't know or care how much drink I spilled as I kept jumping until I finally landed on top of the bar counter. What I hadn't been aware of was that, after I had first jumped onto my own table, a lady who I didn't know had done exactly the same thing at the opposite side of the bar. She also jumped across the table tops until she met me at the bar counter. It was the distraction I needed, as once we met we started head banging together on the counter. Looking at my new wild dancing partner going through her moves had me doubled over with laughter and made me forget about the ignorant landlord. Liz said she was not impressed with my behaviour, and wouldn't be in a hurry to go out locally with me again.

Our Wedding

On the morning of our wedding, Friday, 2nd June 2000, I suppose I had all the same thoughts and fears as any other groom. I was excited, nervous, sad and happy. It was still only 9am, so I decided I would go into my brother Edmund for a chat and a cup of tea.

Edmund had been off the drink and sober for the previous three weeks – as he said himself, he wanted to be in good form and looking well and to do me proud on my big day. When I opened his door, I was shocked and saddened to see Edmund was lying in his bed. drunk as a skunk. On his locker was a large pandy he used for drinking out of, and it was half full of poitin. There were another two bottles of poitin sitting on the floor, one of which was almost empty and the other untouched.

Edmund had been in my house until well past midnight the previous night and must have started drinking after he returned to his own home. When he then asked me why I wasn't working and where was Liz, I knew he had completely forgotten it was our wedding day. I decided I wouldn't remind him, for the time being at least. I wanted to go to my parents and my nephew Joseph's graves, so I hoped he might be sobered up a bit by the time I got back.

That morning, standing at my parent's grave, I cried my eyes out. It was the day that they would have both prayed and wished for, to see me sober at last, and marrying Liz, who was and would be my rock and the steady hand I needed. I was so sad that they were not still with me that morning, but deep down I also knew that they would be watching over us.

Our Wedding

Back at home, I went in again to check on Edmund, hoping he had sobered up a bit, but he was now well into his second bottle, and he was so busy enjoying his own company that he still hadn't remembered it was our wedding day, nor had he remembered talking to me earlier, because he asked me again had I no work to go to and where was Liz.

I knew it was pointless at this stage trying to get him sobered up, so after sitting with him for a while and having the craic, I made some excuse about having to leave. At this stage, the best thing for both of us was for Edmund to stay in his bed that day, and hopefully not remember about our wedding until it was all over. Before I left I opened his bottle of poitin and filled up his pandy, with a lot of emotions racing through my mind. I picked up the full pandy of poitin myself, and winking at Edmund I said, "Cheers, Brother," and took a good mouthful. Edmund stared up at me in disbelief and said, "Go easy on that stuff wee brother, and anyway you shouldn't be drinking as you can't handle it like me". I passed it back again to Edmund, and he put it up to his mouth and drank the rest of it.

I knew then by the amount Edmund had drunk that he certainly wouldn't remember our wedding that day, or anything else for that matter. When I drank that mouthful of poitin that morning I was definitely playing with fire – it certainly was another close shave for me and another second of madness that could have destroyed my life. It was sad enough for my brother Edmund to miss my wedding, without me, the groom, also making a mess of things.

I shudder now to think of how close I came to drinking that morning. After I got over those bad few moments, I was okay and thinking straight again. I had been planning and looking forward to getting us all together that day and getting a family photo, but I now knew for certain that we had missed a wonderful opportunity to have us all together and dressed as best we could. Although my parents were gone, and we never did get a complete family photo, I thought it would be nice to have myself, my two brothers and two sisters pictured together.

When it was my turn to make my speech, my mind went completely blank and I could not remember who I was supposed to thank and give a mention to. I was nervous and also concerned about Edmund's wellbeing and the fact he wasn't present. I stood up with the mike in my hand and with all these thoughts going through my mind. After a few moments silence, I did manage to compose myself and thank the right people, including and most importantly, my new beautiful bride.

All in all, our wedding day went very well and everyone, including Liz and myself, thoroughly enjoyed themselves. It was about 5am before we finally arrived home in Carrigart. As Liz and I weren't drinking, we both ended up coming home on our wedding night in separate cars. Liz drove one of our guest's cars and I drove our own. Back in our house, as we were preparing to lock up, we could hear Edmund singing loud and clear as he made his way towards our door. On entering our house Edmund put his arm around me and says, "It won't be long now brother to the big shindig". When I then informed him that he had actually missed our wedding, he looked at me in disbelief. I knew Edmund was genuinely gutted as he turned with his head down, and walked back into his home in silence.

For our honeymoon, we travelled to Washington, D.C. USA to visit Liz's relatives. On arrival, we got the great news that we were going to get a special visit of both the United States Capitol building and the White House. The United States Capitol in Washington, D.C. is among the most impressive and important buildings in the world. The Senate and the House of Representatives have met there for more than two centuries. It is a working office building as well as a tourist attraction and is visited by millions every year. The Capitol also houses an important collection of American art.

On entering the Capitol, we were put through a rigorous security search before finally gaining admission. We were then ushered into a large room where the late Edward 'Teddy' Kennedy, and various other dignitaries were speaking; we were told that they were passing a new government bill.

After that, we made our way to the White House for our next very special tour. The White House is the official residence and principal workplace of the President of the United States. It has been the residence of every U.S. president since John Adams in 1800. After producing our passports for security at the main entrance, we had to wait then for forty-five minutes before we got the all-clear to enter. Once again we were thoroughly searched and scanned by security. Our tour guide was a personal friend of one of Liz's friends, so we got an excellent tour of the entire building inside and out. When our tour guide heard that Liz and I were on our honeymoon he asked me how was married life? Being the character I was, I replied that we were still together anyway, so it was so far so good.

We then travelled onto Pittsburgh to visit friends and from there we got a return flight into Orlando, Florida and spent three days at the Walt Disney World Resort theme park – the most visited complex of its kind in the world. On our return to Pittsburgh, we then continued travelling and visited Chicago, Virginia, Philadelphia, Atlantic City and New York. We used the Grey Hound bus service for most of our journey and I remember as we were travelling I was able to connect the names of several places with country and western songs.

Becoming Very Unsettled in Life

Even though I was aware how blessed I was to have Liz in my life I had become very restless and unsettled. I had everything in Liz, whom I loved so much, but my old reckless character was coming back to haunt me. I was still sober, but I could take a mad notion, and on the spur of the moment I could book myself a flight into some city. It wasn't unusual for me to land in Glasgow, Newcastle, Liverpool or London on my own. I might not be very long back home when I would take off again.

One weekend Liz and myself had arranged to go shopping in Belfast, and on the Friday morning before we left home I decided on impulse I would travel on to Cardiff, Wales that evening. I told Liz my intention, and although she was concerned, she was familiar with my unpredictable and restless personality. Even though I didn't have any friends there to visit, I thought I would like to spend a weekend there and see what kind of a town it was.

Later that same evening I arrived at Belfast International airport, and discovered that the flight had already left for Cardiff. The lady at the check-in desk told me my next best option was to fly into Bristol, and get the train from there. After I arrived into Bristol train station, I went to purchase my ticket to Cardiff, and the gentleman at the ticket desk asked me was I over for the rugby. It was about 7pm. I hadn't a clue what he was on about, so I asked him who was playing, and where. He then informed me Wales were playing France that same evening in Cardiff.

After hearing that unexpected piece of information, I said to him "That could make it difficult for me getting accommodation".

My travel guide told me that unless I had someplace booked, then I hadn't a hope in hell.

Since I was trying to figure out my options, I asked him, "What kind of a town is Bristol?"

He answered, "It's a good town, but it's also very busy tonight and probably booked out as well".

I then said to him, "Then could you recommend another town to me where I might get a bed, as I don't have all night to be wandering about".

As he was looking at me, I was thinking to myself, "He will be wondering what kind of a loony I am".

He said to me, "What about Weston-Super-Mare?" I said I had never heard of such a place, but I liked the name, and then asked, "How far away is that?"

My travel guide told me it was a very popular holiday resort on the coast, about a half-an-hour away by train journey. Well I figured there wouldn't be too many tourists about in April, but nevertheless I had to go someplace for the night. I bought myself a ticket and made my way to catch my train. Liz rang me to see how I was getting on, and whether I had arrived in Cardiff. I had to explain that there was a change of plan and direction, and that I was now on a train going to Weston-Super-Mare. Like myself, Liz had never heard of it before, so it took me some time convincing her I was still sober, and hadn't hit the bottle again.

I did seriously begin to question my own sanity afterwards. I was at the age when most of my schoolmates were grandparents, and as I was sober I should have more sense than to land in some strange town all alone. I had everything and more than I ever needed at home, so what running about was I at anyway?

Drinking Again

I was now 8 years sober, but for quite some time I had been toying with the idea of having another drink. I had this crazy notion that I wanted to prove to myself that I could have another drink, and stop again of my own free will. I would then be able to say that I enjoyed my last drink. I hadn't talked to anyone about my plan. I had my mind made up, so I suppose I didn't want anyone trying to talk me out of it.

I purposely went to London for a weekend on my own to have my drink. It was like the old saying that a criminal will always return to the scene of the crime. Although I knew I was on my way to drink, I decided I wouldn't have any in the airport or on the short plane journey. Even though I was excited and wanting a drink I was also very nervous about the consequences. I suppose I was trying to convince myself that this time would be different and I wouldn't make a pig out of myself.

I arrived at my hotel in London as planned and ordered myself a pint. It was a strange experience, and I seemed to be away in a trance. Every time I finished a drink, I would go to the toilets to see if I was still sober and steady on my feet. After five or six drinks, I wasn't worried how I was, so I started phoning old drinking buddies and former housemates and made my way up to the Windmill pub in Acton.

That first night went according to plan, but once I awoke the following morning I was back to square one again. I hadn't the patience to take the time to have a shave or a shower and without any breakfast I went in search of a drink. When the social drinkers were coming out for a good night on the town, I was completely out of my head and had to retire for the night. The following day I was going home to Liz and I didn't want her to know I had been drinking. Although my form was bad, I fought against my urges to go for the cure, and made it home. I foolishly assumed that everything went sort of okay. Back into my routine at home, I wasn't tempted to drink, but I knew that when the urge would come on I would plan another weekend away.

Some months later, I got the craving and the urge once again to have another drink. I figured I had managed it sort of okay in London the last time. In fact, I believed I would even control it much better this time. One time an addiction councillor asked me what would make me drink again. My answer was simply, "If I want a drink bad enough then I will drink". Well, now I wanted that drink, and once again I decided to get away on my own.

I made an appointment with my doctor as I wanted to get a sick cert. I wanted some time off work and the cert would sort that out. Also, I would be able to sign on and not lose out financially. When I went for my appointment, I was disappointed to discover my own doctor was off on holidays. His replacement didn't know my form, but I figured I wouldn't have any bother in putting on a good act, and bluffing her.

When I complained of severe backache, the doctor asked how much pain I was in. I said "Doctor you know nothing about it. I haven't slept in three nights." After a struggle to get me up on her examining couch, she returned with a large needle. I didn't want a needle stuck in my arse, but I had no option other than to play along. After giving me the unwanted injection, she declared me unfit for three days. But I wasn't happy with that, and I said to her "Doctor, if you don't give me a cert for at least a week, I won't receive any money from the social welfare". As the doctor was rewriting my cert, she asked me to explain a little bit about my lifestyle, so I start off telling her about some of the crazy situations I had got myself into. She seemed really amused, and she said, "Martin Jim, if you stopped your ducking and diving, and put your energy and brain into something worthwhile, I have no doubt you could be quite successful".

When she then told me the injection should help to ease my pain, I said "Doctor, my back is now fine, but my arse is throbbing". She laughed at that, shook my hand, and wished me luck.

This time I decided to go to Newcastle to have my drink, as I was very aware that I could get into trouble should I go drinking around my own local bars. Once I returned home, Liz nor anyone else would be any the wiser. Once I got checked in at Belfast International Airport, I started drinking, and swallowed a good few more on the short flight.

After I arrived into Newcastle, I immediately went off on a serious bender and straight back to my old alcoholic ways. Some days later, I left Newcastle and landed in Liverpool; from Liverpool I made my way back home to Carrigart.

Although Liz did pick me up at the airport, she told me she couldn't cope with my drinking and disappearing acts any longer. She told me that she was leaving me and I knew she was serious. I was wrecked from my binge drinking, and I was too ill to beg her to give me another chance.

After we arrived back at our home in Carrigart, I put on my bedroom slippers and was preparing for the horrors that awaited me. Liz was on the phone and she came in and told me that we were going up to visit my sister Bridie. I didn't want to go but Liz insisted, as she said I couldn't be trusted to be left alone. To keep the peace, I reluctantly got into the car, but as we were driving up the road, I noticed a car parked outside a holiday home. I knew the couple who owned it, and I also knew I would get a drink in this same house.

Drinking Again

I told Liz to stop the car, and I jumped out and landed in the house still wearing my bedroom slippers. The lady of the house said she was so disappointed I had gone back on the drink. Liz came in to rescue me, but I had already swallowed two large glasses of whiskey and was looking for more. My host advised me to go and sleep it off, but that was then the last thing on my mind.

After going home and changing into my shoes, I went on tour again. Some days later I landed in Glasgow, and after drinking throughout the night, I hopped on a train for Newcastle. During that bender I remember finding myself in Leeds, with no recollection whatsoever of why or how I travelled there.

In Leeds railway station, I discovered I had lost my wallet, which also contained my passport. I reported my loss to the police and gave them my mobile number should they need to make contact. I didn't have much hope of being reunited with my prized documents. I was feeling wrecked, paranoid and anxious to return home. I knew I needed valid photographic ID for security at the airport, so I went and had my photo taken in a passport booth before purchasing a seven day railway ticket in Leeds railway station. I now had my railway ticket, complete with my photograph attached and although I knew it wasn't the requested form of ID. I decided I would make my way to the airport and hope for the best.

I sure was relieved when my makeshift ID was accepted by the airport staff and, as I was departing Belfast airport, I was surprised when I received a call from the police in Leeds informing me that my wallet had been handed into the station. The policeman requested I call into their station to collect it and I told him it wouldn't be possible, as I was now in Belfast airport on my way home. The police man seemed amused, since he was aware I was without my passport and he laughed when I told him about my temporary ID. I then asked him would he be so kind and post my wallet to my home address and that he would find my full postal address on my passport. He did as requested and three days later the postman reunited me with my parcel.

It was another blessing that Liz decided to listen to the song 'Stand by your Man' by Tammy Wynette. Although I should have known better, I have to admit that for a short period during that time I wrongly assumed I could get away with what I was doing. I just thought that once in a while I would go off some place on my own and have my wee drink. I suppose I also thought I was enjoying myself. But in reality, once I took that first sip, I was completely powerless and the craving I had for a drink was unreal. After I returned home from those binges, it was pretty much the same pattern with the same suffering both mentally and physically afterwards. I also felt so guilty for disappearing on Liz, and putting her through endless worry and turmoil. As I came to terms with my situation I felt so stupid for making the same mistakes over and over again.

I was back at home and was at my work, and everything was going well again, but I knew in my heart I was going to drink again. I was just biding my time, and waiting for the right opportunity or excuse. It came when I was admitted to the day surgery ward of Altnagelvin Hospital, Derry, to have my varicose veins removed from both legs. I was allowed home later that same evening. My doctor said they were the worse veins he had ever seen. They were damaged when I had my accident in 1986.

Some days after my operation I was at home recovering, and the bandage covering my left leg and skin graft was a bit tight. I was concerned that it might break the delicate skin so I got myself a pair of scissors and cut the bandage off. That stunt would have certainly been against doctor's orders. I was bored being laid up at home, and thought my circumstances sort of justified having a drink. I decided I would go down to my mate Joe in Dublin. My legs were still sore and badly bruised and I still had the bandage on my right leg, so I suppose the four hour bus journey each way wasn't a good idea.

Drinking Again

As I walked to Joe's flat, I felt pretty cold, so I went into an off-licence and bought a bottle of whiskey, figuring I would treat myself to a few hot whiskeys. I would just take it easy on the drink, and sure, a few nice hot drinks would only heat me up. Again, that was wishful thinking, and after finishing the bottle, I got myself a taxi into the city centre and went on a pub crawl. My bed for those two nights was a sleeping bag, so I was very lucky I didn't do a serious injury to my legs during that session. Even though I didn't follow my doctor's orders, I am glad to add that my operation proved to be successful.

On another occasion I was admitted to hospital after I had been feeling unwell for sometime, but was assuming that it was only a bad dose of the 'flu. My x-ray showed a large scar on my lung. All sorts of thoughts were going through my mind. I thought I might have cancer and that I could be goosed. That night, as I lay in my hospital bed, I was thinking on lots of different scenarios. If my time had come, then I could accept it. I figured that, as I didn't have any children depending on me, I wasn't leaving anyone in a bad predicament. I had no doubt that my beautiful wife would have no problem in getting herself another man should she ever need some loving, but I thought she would have trouble finding another character like me.

Some days later I was relieved when my doctor told me it was, in fact, pneumonia. Although it was great news for me, my heart went out to some other patients in my ward whose news wasn't as good. Your life can be going so well and you can just take a lot of things for granted, but in a couple of short seconds that could suddenly change. You can receive news in a short sentence, or in a phone call that will blow your world apart.

I had been sober again for some time and Liz liked planning short city breaks for us on a regular basis. It was something for us both to look forward to, and I suppose Liz was trying to keep me from getting bored and restless. We had a peculiar incident in a hotel in Glasgow city centre. On the three separate occasions we stayed there, we were evacuated each time in the middle of the night due to the fire alarm going off. I remember joking to the gentleman at reception when we were checking in on our third visit about our two previous experiences. He seemed amused, and he looked at me, and said "Well if it goes off again, we will come looking for you". That night we couldn't believe it when the dreaded alarm bell rang, and for the third time in a row we had to evacuate.

On another occasion we were holidaying in Lake Garda, Italy. We decided we would go to Milan for a day's sightseeing. I had this mental vision of it being packed with beautiful women, who would be strutting about and modelling their stuff. Arriving into Milan railway station, we discovered there was a very large police presence patrolling the area with guard dogs. I was surprised and thought to myself, "This is either a good or bad thing".

Shortly afterwards, as we were walking down a street, I noticed a character on the opposite side, and for some strange reason, I got a bad feeling about him and the area we were now in. I told Liz we would cross and go down another street, and while doing so I noticed our friend was tailing us from a distance. I didn't say anything to Liz as I didn't want to alarm her, so I suggested we go into a café for something to eat. I was figuring it would give me a chance to weigh up the situation.

We sat at a corner table, and I couldn't see any sight of our follower. I then watched as four fellows sat down at the table next to us. I noticed they hadn't bought any food, and it made me wary, and almost certain they were on our case. I still hadn't said anything to Liz, but before we finished our food, I suddenly said, "Let's get out of here". I jumped up from our table, grabbed Liz's hand, and raced outside.

As we ran across busy rows of traffic, trying to get back into the train station, I noticed the men in hot pursuit. I prayed hard to

Drinking Again

my friend St Anthony to protect us. Thank God we did manage to get safely back onto our train. One of the gang followed us into our carriage. He was wearing a white shirt, which had several old blood stains on it, and he looked a dangerous piece of work. It was the first experience that Liz and I had had of being in a dangerous situation, and I must admit we were both frightened.

Back at our hotel in Lake Garda, I mentioned the incident to the manager. He said that particular area could be pretty dangerous, but once you got out of there it was okay. I said, "This morning we told you we were going to visit Milan. It's a pity you didn't think of warning us first".

Since that day was really hot, I was wearing a sort of muscle top vest because I wanted to catch as much sun as possible. It's possible that I stood out a bit from the crowd, and the fact that I have several large scars on my arms most likely gave the impression that I was a real thug or a football hooligan.

The Death of My Brother Edmund

I was in my home having a cup of tea, and Edmund walked into my kitchen. Living next door to Edmund meant I knew most of his moves. Looking at him that morning, I knew he was in really bad form and that he had been on a binge. Edmund asked me if I had a few moments to spare. I told him I had and I followed him into his mobile home.

Edmund's problem that morning was a forty-ounce bottle of whiskey that he could not get opened; this particular bottle had an unusual cork, which was now broken. I went back again to my own kitchen for a corkscrew, and when I handed Edmund the now-opened bottle, he put his arm around me and said "Everybody needs a wee brother". Little did I know those would be Edmund's last words.

Edmund was in a deep sleep when I entered sometime later, and, as always, I stood by his bedside watching and listening to him for a few minutes to make sure he was still breathing, and to try to make sure his head was propped up with a few pillows. Looking at Edmund in that drunken, comatose state was really hard, and it sure did bring home to me the devastation of alcohol abuse. It was heart-breaking to watch, and I thought of how many times our family witnessed me in the same sad state.

On Monday, 5th September 2005, I went in again to check on Edmund. When I opened his bedroom door, I was shocked when

The Death of My Brother Edmund

I found my brother lying on the floor. I knew at first glance he was dead. Although we had been talking several times about such a scenario, one is never really prepared when it actually happens. I knelt down on the floor beside Edmund and said a prayer. I cried my eyes out as I closed his eyes and covered his body with a blanket.

When I went outside, I stopped again. Although I was certain Edmund was dead, I had to go back in to confirm it in my mind. I carried out that same procedure several times before I was confident enough to break the sad news to my family.

People might think that, with my own alcoholism and struggles, I should have known better than to open the bottle for Edmund that morning, but in hindsight I would probably still do the same thing. Edmund needed a drink that morning and hadn't made a decision to try and get sober; if I was in Edmund's position, I would have expected him to do the same for me. Edmund had often said to me that he hoped he would have a sudden death, and not end up in a nursing home, dependent on its care. I suppose Edmund was well aware of the fact that sometimes a patient in a nursing home, or indeed a hospital, can get neglected. Edmund died from a condition known as Sarcoidosis. It was not at all alcohol related, which was strange and somewhat comforting.

Edmund had a talent and gift for life that sadly lost out to the demon drink, and we will never know what might have been. Edmund used to write poems and songs about events and daily happenings in his life. It was no bother to him to put an air to these same songs and to sing them in the local pubs. He didn't keep a book for such writing and he just wrote them off the top of his head on whatever paper was available at the time. I found his songs written on toilet paper, calendars, cardboard boxes and all sorts of pieces and scraps of paper. As you can imagine a lot of what and who he wrote about can't be published, as he did not mince his words and wasn't afraid of naming and shaming people. A few people had threatened to sue, but as Edmund once said to me, "Sure, they're wasting their time as everything I wrote is true."

At Edmund's funeral Mass, the priest and our cousin Moira read out two of his poems. The first one had everyone in tears and the second poem had all of us laughing. There was a large crowd present and they all clapped, giving a huge round of applause. The choir sang the song 'Wine into Water', which was very appropriate. Edmund's funeral was certainly different and he sure did get the send-off he fully deserved.

As I was later sorting out Edmund's personal items, I found the whiskey bottle I had opened for him that morning; it was lying in his bed, and it was almost empty. It's hard to imagine the devastation that alcohol can bring unless you witness it on a personal level. Looking at that almost empty bottle, I figured that before Edmund had died he would not have suffered physically or mentally due to the large amount of whiskey he had consumed. That thought alone helped to ease my hurt a little. If I thought he had been lying alone in the horrors prior to his death, it would have been a much worse feeling for me.

From an early age, Edmund was my hero and I idolised and loved him so much. He sure was a character in life and it now seems he got his wish of a sudden death.

When my brother Edmund died, one of his mates had just been on a huge bender; like all of us, he was gutted. He was going through the horrors and just wasn't able to come to Edmund's wake. His own brother had been trying to get him to come with him, so they could both pay their respects, but our friend was in no shape or form to attend. On the morning of Edmund's funeral, his brother once again approached him and pleaded, "Now you know you can't miss Edmund Jim's funeral". Our friend looked up at his brother and replied, "I'm not fit today, but you go on without me, and tell Edmund I'll be over to see him when I get myself straightened out". When I was told that story, I laughed but it also brought home to me the devastation that alcohol can have on both body and mind. Alcoholic-related stories can be both humorous and sad.

This reminds me of a similar incident that happened to me when I was drinking. I was walking along the road one day on my way to some pub, and I was in the horrors. A neighbour came along in his car and gave me a lift. It so happened this same gentleman had just buried his mother the previous day, and I had attended the wake. As we were travelling in his car, my alcoholic-soaked brain was so confused that I turned and asked the driver, "How is your mother keeping now?" The fact that I had just been at the poor lady's wake a few days earlier must have brought her into my mind, but it didn't register with me at the time that she was in fact dead. Strangely enough, after I had asked the question it did come back to me, but the harm was done. It was so embarrassing. I apologised immediately and my neighbour was okay about it and said he understood.

Hopefully My Last Drink

Five months after Edmund's death, I had what I hope and pray will be my last drink. I landed in Newcastle alone, and I went off on a serious bender. I had to book and pay for a total of three separate return flights before I finally got home; I also left my luggage behind. Although I knew I was doing wrong, I just couldn't stop once I got the taste of it.

When I finally made it home to Carrigart, Liz's friend Rose came out to meet us and talk to me and offer Liz her support. I was a complete nervous wreck, and every single thought that came into my mind depressed and worried me. I needed a drink badly that night and I asked Liz and Rose to take me to a hotel that I knew would be quiet. I promised Liz before we left that I had once again made the decision of quitting the drink, and that I wouldn't let her down.

At closing time I was craving another binge, but thank God I listened to Liz and Rose and went home with them. Even though the drink had settled me temporarily, I still tossed and turned most of the night in our bed. I was raving and imagining all sorts of nightmare situations. The following morning I called my doctor and asked for his help. He prescribed for me a few days' supply of Librium tablets. With my addictive personality, I wanted to be sure I had a good supply, so I got another supply from another source, and I never made them aware of my first fix. I was very aware that there were no quick-fix cures, but I was hoping the tablets would help ease some of the horrors and paranoia that awaited me.

Hopefully My Last Drink

The next few days and nights were horrific, and the power went from my legs completely. I was confined to bed, and this time I was genuinely certified unfit for my work. I regained the power in my legs some days later and returned to work and got back into my sober routine.

While I was living in London I got to know a gentleman who ended up on the streets due to his alcoholism. Although the publicans refused to serve him, he would come in and ask the customers present for the price of a few cans of beer. I always made a point of treating him with respect and dignity, and one day he told me the circumstances surrounding his downfall. This same gentleman had been a very successful businessman with a beautiful wife and family, and he was also a pioneer. One evening as he returned home from his work he discovered his home was on fire; the emergency crews were there, but, alas, it was all in vain. His wife and children died in the fire, and his home was completely gutted. He wept uncontrollably as he told me, and said afterwards he just gave up the will to live, and took to the drink as a result. It just proves how easily your life and your circumstances can suddenly change, and how you could lose a grip on your senses.

BOOK THREE

My Spiritual Journey Begins

I was clearing out my attic space, when I came upon an old red biscuit tin that contained personal stuff belonging to my father. There were receipts, etc., as old as fifty years plus, but also inside this same box I discovered a crumpled piece of paper. After straightening it out, I realised it had a picture of St Anthony and the Baby Jesus on one side. On the reverse was written the number seven, and it had these instructions:

> How can we become clients of St Anthony? The answer is given in quotations from one of the greatest clients of the Saint, Pope Leo XIII.
>
> 1. It is not enough that you love St Anthony, said Pope Leo, but you must also make him loved.
>
> 2. Invoke his assistance.
>
> There are various ways in which Pope Leo's second rule may be carried out, for example:
>
> - Recite daily some prayer in St Anthony's honour.
> - Have a little altar of the Saint, or carry his picture, statuette, medal or scapular.
> - Visit his shrine on Tuesday.

From an early age I remember my mother had several prayer books with a plastic band holding them together. They were worn and damaged from many years of use. One of these books was the Nine Tuesday Novena to St Anthony. This was most likely my first introduction to this saint. Finding that piece of paper proved that both my parents must have had a devotion to St Anthony and it certainly increased my love, devotion and interest in this remarkable saint.

St Anthony

St Anthony was born in Lisbon, Portugal. The exact date of St Anthony's birth is not known reliably, but it is now thought he was born around the year 1190 (this is estimated from his probable age of forty at his death, from scientific analysis of his skeleton). His father Martin and his mother, Maria, christened him Fernando Martins (I was pleased to discover I shared the same forename as his father). Like St Francis, he was born into a wealthy family. His parents belonged to one of the prominent families of the city, and wished for him to live a worldly life of luxury and comfort. But Fernando felt called as a young man to a spiritual life, and entered the religious order of St Augustine. "Whoever enters a monastery," he later wrote, "goes, so to speak, to his grave".

He knew his parents were not happy about him joining a religious order; nevertheless, he continued with his religious studies. His parents could not let go and visited him so often that he finally decided that if he was to give his life totally to God, he must detach himself entirely from their interference. He requested to be transferred to the Holy Cross Monastery in Coimbra, which was a long journey from Lisbon and was the capital of Portugal at that time. Here he found peace and remained for the next eight years. During that time and especially after his ordination to the priesthood, he dedicated himself to study of Holy Scripture and doing works of charity.

St Francis of Assisi's order had spread throughout Italy and was also established in Spain and his own native Portugal. Fernando liked the humility and poverty of the new Order of St Francis. When he first saw the relics of the Franciscan Martyrs in the city of Coimbra, who had a short time before been put to death, he learned that it was a very dangerous mission trying to convert the Muslims in Africa, by preaching the Catholic faith to them. Nevertheless, he was so inflamed by the thought that good men could be brutally murdered just for preaching the word of Jesus Christ, that he had an ardent desire to go there himself to take up the mantle and continue to preach the Faith about the gentle ways of Jesus Christ and Christianity. With this intention, he became a member of the Franciscan Friars Minor and at the age of twenty-five he received the full habit in the Monastery of St Anthony, thus prompting him to take the name of Anthony.

Anthony then asked to go to Africa, hoping to take over where the Martyrs had left off, and finally persuaded his superiors to allow him to go. But shortly after he reached his destination, disaster befell him when he was struck by an unknown virus. This left him powerless to walk and travel out to the area's most in need of the faith from where no preacher had ever returned. Others commented at the time that perhaps the Lord had a greater plan for Anthony, other than Martyrdom at such a young age. He was obliged to return home when his condition hadn't improved after a number of months. He, of course, intended going back as soon as he was well, but fate once again intervened when, during the voyage home, a violent storm arose and they became shipwrecked off the coast of Sicily.

Fate seemed to take a hand once more when the Provincial of the Province that he was attached to, asked him to go to the Monastery of Montepaolo in Forli to celebrate Mass for the lay brothers there. After a time as Chaplain to the hermitage in Montepaolo, Anthony's preaching ability was discovered at an ordination service, when he was commanded to speak under obedience – the superior not expecting anything remarkable.

He travelled tirelessly in both Northern Italy and Southern France, going to cities where there was a lot of poverty and crime, to preach to people greatly in need of God in their life and trying to convert the non-believers. People from all walks of life, both rich and poor, came to listen to his uplifting words. Town squares were packed when he came to a town and gave a talk. If the town square was not big enough, farmers would give him the use of their fields to accommodate the large crowd. It is recorded that where the Saint's words or advice could not help a person in great need, he worked a miracle for them. It is written that crowds of over ten thousand often gathered to hear him preach and it was also recorded that without any amplification, people at the back of a huge crowd could hear his words as clearly as those at the front.

All throughout Lent 1231, St Anthony preached to ever-increasing crowds in Padua, Italy, but his preaching and the endless hours of confessions left him prostrate. Around this time, St Anthony had a premonition of his approaching death. The Friars invited St Anthony to go to Camposampiero, a town twenty kilometres from Padua, so that he might recover his strength. In St Anthony's day, it was a village which housed the castle of Count Tiso IV. The Count had been an unscrupulous politician, but after hearing St Anthony preach he was converted, and donated a plot of land to the Friars, on which a hermitage was built. The ground was damp at this time of year, and it aggravated St Anthony's illness. This problem was solved when the Friars noticed St Anthony admire an immense walnut tree on the property. They told Count Tiso about it, and he had a small tree house built in the walnut tree for St Anthony. It was also during this time in Camposampiero that St Anthony had his vision of the Child Jesus (most statues of St Anthony have the Child Jesus resting in his arms). In remembrance of these two facts, there are two churches in Camposampiero: the shrine of the

Walnut Tree and the shrine of the Vision. The original church in Camposampiero was dedicated to St John the Baptist.

The care of Count Tiso and the Friars was not enough to bring St Anthony back to health. On June 13th 1231, St Anthony came down from his tree house to eat the noonday meal with the Friars. They had scarcely begun when he collapsed into their arms. As the Friars supported him he whispered to them, "If you think it is all right, let us return to Padua. I love Padua, where God has worked so many wonders and conversions through my poor preaching! I want to die there".

The Friars put him into a cart and travelled toward Padua, but St Anthony was already too weak to make it. As they approached the Poor Clare's Convent in Arcella, a town close to Padua, they decided it would be best to take him in there. Sadly they carried him to a chair and tried to make him comfortable. Friar Roger held St Anthony's head, because his lungs were filling with water. His breathing was faint, and after receiving the Sacrament of Confession and Absolution, he began to sing the hymn to the Blessed Mother, 'O Glorious Lady'. As he finished, raising his eyes to Heaven with a look of ecstasy, he stared straight ahead. When his fellow Friar, who was holding him, asked what he saw, he replied, "Video Dominum Meum". Translated it means "I See My Lord". St Anthony then peacefully passed away on Friday 13th June 1231.

The Friars carried St Anthony's body the one mile distance from Arcella to Padua, where his tomb still remains. The miracles associated with St Anthony during his short life were redoubled after his death. On May 30th, 1232, less than a year after his death, Pope Gregory canonised St Anthony of Padua. St Anthony is the Patron Saint associated with the return of lost things and missing persons. He is petitioned for help in finding almost everything that is lost, from car keys and misplaced papers to a lost job, a lost lover, or a straying partner. People who are regarded as lost souls may also be placed in his care. Because St Anthony travelled widely, he is also appealed to for safe travel. St Anthony is known as the Saint of miracles, so I suppose that title covers pretty much everything.

St Anthony's Nine Tuesday's Novena

The history and devotion of the Nine Tuesday's novena is attributed to the fact that the burial of St Anthony took place on a Tuesday. It was not, however, until almost four hundred years after the death of St Anthony that the special novena of Nine Successive Tuesdays was recommended by St Anthony himself. The occasion was as follows – according to an authentic document, which is included in the life of the Saint.

In the year 1617, a lady of rank, being full of confidence in St Anthony, visited the church of his order at Bologna, Northern Italy and prostrating herself before his altar, prayed fervently for the gift of a child. She was assured, by a strange sense of interior consolation, that her prayer had been heard. During the following night she beheld the Saint in a dream, and heard him say to her, "O woman, for nine consecutive Tuesdays, pray before my image, and what you pray for you shall obtain". This lady performed the novena according to these directions, and immediately upon the close of it had evidence that she had obtained the blessing which had been promised as her reward. To her great joy she gave birth after 22 years of childless marriage. However, her child was badly deformed. But even in this her faith did not fail, and she brought the baby to the shrine and sought St Anthony's help again. Soon afterwards, the child was found to be normal and whole. The story of this miracle helped to spread the practise of this devotion throughout Italy and the novena of Nine Tuesdays in honour of St Anthony of Padua immediately spread over all Europe. Sometimes I now wait until a Tuesday if I have an important decision to make.

Every year, millions of pilgrims from all over the world visit the Basilica of St Anthony in Padua, which for over seven centuries has contained the remains of St Anthony. Liz and myself had the privilege on several occasions of visiting this very special shrine, and there is so much for the pilgrim to do and see. It was fascinating, and a dream come true for us, to join the endless queue of devotees who come with their sufferings, hopes, and also in thanksgiving for favours received from this great saint and miracle worker.

We also visited the former Poor Clare's Convent in Arcella where St Anthony died and that meant so much to me. Although frequently damaged by fire and bombs throughout the centuries, it was always quickly restored. The cell where St Anthony died is now preserved inside a large church built in 1895, on the original ancient foundations. There is a life-size statue of St Anthony in the actual spot where he died. It is known as The Cell of the Passing Away.

On one of our trips to Padua, we were browsing through the shops and I noticed a beautiful bottle, which had a picture inside it of St Anthony and Baby Jesus. It certainly was an unusual bottle, but being alcoholic I suppose all bottles catch my eye. Coincidentally, this same bottle contained a clear alcohol. I bought it, and then I went inside the Basilica and touched St Anthony's tomb with it. Sitting there at the tomb, I was deep in thought, contemplating the future, and all possible scenarios. Looking at my bottle, I figured if I could remain sober then I had no other fear in life, and could possibly cope and accept whatever might come my way. When we returned home from that particular trip, I placed my bottle on a corner shelf in our bedroom. Every time I look at that bottle it reminds me of the devastation of my alcoholic binges.

On another occasion in Padua, I had St Anthony's last words 'Video Dominum Meum' inscribed on the top of my right arm. Each time I look at my personal inscription it gives me a somewhat comforting feeling. During our latest pilgrimage to St Anthony's

My Spiritual Journey Begins

tomb, Liz and I visited Camposampiero, which is only a twenty minute train journey from Padua. It was wonderful to visit these two beautiful churches/shrines of the Walnut Tree and the Vision of the Child Jesus.

To complete our personal spiritual journey with St Anthony, Liz and I arrived in Lisbon, Portugal, the city of his birth. A beautiful church is now built on the site of St Anthony's home, and there is a stairway leading underneath the church, which leads you into St Anthony's bedroom and the actual site of his birth.

Although the city of Lisbon was destroyed by an earthquake and fire on 1st November 1755 (All Saints' Day), the room that St Anthony was born in survived. We were booked into a hotel within walking distance, and Liz and myself both got so much peace and satisfaction from sitting in the room in which our beloved saint was born. Somehow I knew I had to visit there. After some time. Liz and the other people who were present decided they would go upstairs to Mass, and I suppose I was pleased that I now had the room to myself. I don't know how long I stayed there before I decided to leave and make my way upstairs to find Liz, but when I went to open the door I discovered I was locked in. The staff on duty must have assumed I had also left at the same time as Liz, so I was now locked inside St Anthony's bedroom. Instead of panicking, I somehow felt so happy and at peace. I also felt it was St Anthony's way of letting me know he was happy with my presence there and wanted my company. I did manage to get out eventually, and was reunited with Liz.

At home I got a great desire to get a large statue of St Anthony for our home. I thought it would be really personal to create my own little shrine. During my previous visit to Padua, I had seen beautiful statues of St Anthony in all sizes in the shop adjoining St

Anthony's Basilica. I knew it would make it more special to travel to Padua and take our statue from there. By doing this I could have it blessed by the Friars and also have it touch his tomb. Before we planned our journey, I contacted the staff associated with the shop and they assured me they would have a statue ready for us. They advised me to contact the airlines as they didn't know what their policy was in carrying such a large and personal object. We were travelling with Ryanair and, although they have strict guidelines, I decided not to bother asking in advance.

Liz and myself arrived in Padua and the Friars had St Anthony's statue out on display for us. It was life-size and complete with the Child Jesus resting in his arms. It was the most beautiful statue of St Anthony/Child Jesus we had ever seen. Liz and I both loved it. The Friars blessed our statue and helped us carry it inside the adjoining Basilica and had it touch his tomb. At the tomb, we all said a prayer to St Anthony asking for his protection on our return journey home to Carrigart. We then placed our statue inside its original timber box, which was huge; the total weight was 42 kilos. The Friars also had wrapped our statue in bubble wrap and added extra padding inside the box for further protection. They secured the lid of the box with large screws, which they inserted with a cordless drill. We placed our statue on a large trolley and the Friars helped us to transport it the short distance to our hotel.

The following morning, I ordered a large hatchback taxi to take us from Padua to the airport in Venice, which was an hour's drive. On arrival at Venice/Treviso airport, we got a trolley to transport our friend to the check-in area on the second floor. We then discovered our trolley was too big for the lift, but Liz and I managed to lift the box and place it into the lift in an upright position. On arrival at the second floor, we then placed the statue back onto another trolley, and we had an audience as we continued on our way to the check-in desk. I was expecting and prepared to pay a large fee for our precious cargo. The Friars had prepared an e-mail in both Italian and English, confirming St Anthony was indeed inside the box. After the lady at the check-in desk read my e-mail, she smiled and said she would be happy to let us take St Anthony on board for the small fee of £35.

We all arrived into Dublin airport in one piece and again, we had an audience as we steered our trolley through security and customs. We didn't have any problems there and continued on our way outside the terminal to catch our bus for Donegal. When we went to get on board, the driver told us he couldn't accept any cargo from the airport. I told him it was St Anthony, the patron saint of travellers who was inside the box, and I didn't think he would be impressed if he was refused to travel. The driver then changed his mind and said he would love to take us all on board. Although it was a daunting task to attempt, I somehow knew we would succeed, and we all arrived home to Carrigart safe and sound. It was an added bonus or 'coincidence' when I later discovered that the day/date we travelled home with St Anthony was All Saints Day, November 1st.

Receiving My Rosary for the Third Time

Liz asked me if I would go with her to meet a priest who was well known for his healing powers. To be honest, I didn't want to go, but I could understand Liz was worried that I would go back drinking. I agreed to go and was thinking that if it gives Liz peace of mind then it can't be a bad idea.

A few hours later I met Fr Willie Rafferty for the first time. We shook hands and he asked, "How are you, and what do you want me to pray for?"

I replied, "Father I'm fine today, thanks, but I would like you to pray for my wife Liz".

I then told him very honestly about my alcoholism and my restless character, and that I knew Liz was worried I would drink again. Fr Willie Rafferty blessed and prayed over me and asked me to say the Rosary every day. I told him the last time I said the Rosary was when my parents were alive, and I wouldn't know now how to say it. The priest then reached into a plastic bag that contained quite a few Rosaries and gave me one. As well as the beautiful set of beads, there was also a card/booklet with the story of each Mystery and instructions on how to pray the Rosary.

As I held my Rosary in my hand, I got a warm feeling in my heart. I remembered receiving a Rosary from the nun I met as I travelled to London for the first time and, on another occasion, many years later, Bishop Edward Daly presented me with another Rosary. Bishop Daly was the Catholic Lord Bishop of Derry from 1974 to

Receiving My Rosary for the Third Time

1993. The image of the then Fr Daly waving a white handkerchief on Bloody Sunday is famous around the world. I never did use those Rosaries and gave both away.

This was now my third time to receive a Rosary and as I held Fr Willie Rafferty's Rosary in my hand, I knew I was meant to say it, and I was looking forward to it.

When we got home I went into my bedroom. I went down on my knees, and as I prayed my Rosary, my eyes filled with tears. It brought back memories of how important the Rosary was to both my parents, and how much faith and belief they had in it. It also brought back a childhood memory from my school, when one day, our teacher asked us did we believe in God, we all answered yes, so he then asked what made us believe. My classmate Neil stood up, and said, "There are a lot of very intelligent people in this world who have given up their lives to work for God, and they can't all be wrong". I thought that was a very good answer.

Although I was praying to St Anthony, I realised then how I had been taking God and my faith for granted. I had stopped going to Mass, and hadn't been to Confession in years. I knew then that the time had come for me to seriously take a good look at myself, and the lifestyle I was leading. I was truly blessed to have such a wonderful wife in Liz. Although I loved her so much I also had been taking her for granted. How many times I must have hurt her when I went off on my own.

The following day I went to Confessions, and I was slightly embarrassed when the kind priest had to help me through the "Act of Contrition" prayer, as I couldn't remember the exact wording. When I told the priest I had also stopped going to Mass, he continued to explain in a very simple manner, 'God has given us 168 hours every week, and all he asks from us in return is just one hour'.

After coming out of the Confessional box, I felt as if a great weight had been lifted from my shoulders and a feeling of peace as I knelt and prayed the prayers the priest requested.

Liz and I started attending Mass together every Sunday after that. We also started praying the Rosary together on a daily basis, and, as with the Mass, we both received great graces and blessings. I had often heard the old saying that "the families who pray together stay together". From the moment Liz and myself had started praying our Rosary, I developed a strong love and devotion for Our Lady, and a sort of a peace came into my heart and my mind. The urges I had been getting to go away on my own had almost disappeared.

My Spiritual Journey Continues

Our love and devotion to Our Lady then took Liz and myself on another wonderful journey, which brought us to our own very special shrine here in Knock, Co Mayo. We also had the blessings of visiting Fatima, Lourdes, and Medjugorje.

As we made our way to Medjugorje, I thought it was a nice coincidence that the very first apparition in 1981 occurred on 24th June, the feast of St John the Baptist, to whom the church in which St Anthony celebrated his last Mass, and my own parish church is dedicated. Our trip to Medjugorje was also coinciding with the visionary Mirjana Dragicevic being present on Apparition Hill for a public apparition and this very special event was taking place at 10am on the Friday morning.

As usual, they were expecting massive crowds to be present. I talked to Liz and told her I was thinking of camping out overnight on the mountain, as I wanted to be up close to the visionary during the apparition. Liz declined the offer of joining me, and said she would go out with the rest of our group at 6am in the morning. Just after midnight, armed with my blanket, I set off alone on my mission to climb Apparition Hill. I thought it was a small sacrifice to make for such a special event. It certainly proved to me again the power of prayer. After my accident in 1986, I was told I would never walk again. I was also very aware of my gift of sobriety and, of course, my gift of faith. Your faith is also a gift from God. Walking there that night was such a wonderful and special experience and I had the feeling that I was in the place where I was meant to be. Although I was exhausted, I was really enjoying my walk and treasured every moment. Every so often I would just stop and take in the peace and the beauty of the surrounding area.

It was after 2am when I arrived at Our Lady's statue. Quite a number of other pilgrims were already present, and were seated and settled down, waiting for the special moment when Our Lady would appear. I found myself a space in close and next to Our Lady's statue and took up my position. I purposely didn't bring a bottle of water; I knew that if I had to go to the toilet, I would lose my treasured position.

It was a wonderful experience that night, as we all huddled up together on the mountain. I'm fairly certain that most of the other pilgrims present that night were Italians, and even though I didn't know their language, I was happy to pray and sing along. One of them was playing a guitar, and it added to the whole experience. I did try to catch some sleep, and although it was only forty winks, I know I was snoring. I apologised to the lady seated next to me and she just smiled and shook her head.

From 6am the crowds started gathering in huge numbers. Mirjana arrived shortly before 8.30am and the crowd was estimated at ten thousand. People were passing petitions down the mountain, and as I was seated next to Our Lady's statue, I had the privilege of placing them onto it. I had such a good view of Mirjana, and as the crowd prayed and sang along, I was watching closely for the moment Our Lady would appear to her. When the special moment arrived, words could not explain the expression on Mirjana's face, it was at times so happy and peaceful, and other times you could see sadness as Mirjana talked with and listened to Our Lady's message. It certainly was another very memorable occasion for Liz and myself, and the fact that Our Lady is still appearing in Medjugorje during our times makes it extra special.

My cousin Mary arrived home from the USA on her holidays, and she called over to visit us. We were talking about my experiences, and the following day Mary phoned and asked me to call over to her house.

When I arrived, Mary presented me with a beautiful Infant Jesus of Prague statue; it was the gift of a lifetime for me. Mary would have been aware that Jesus was missing from most of my conversation, and it made me aware of how I didn't have a true devotion to the Son of God. It certainly was the link that was missing from my life.

As usual, any chance I got at work I would go into the hospital chapel to say some prayers, and on one of these occasions I found the Holy Cloak novena book to St Joseph, which started me off on a great love, devotion and interest in the life of St Joseph. After all, God chose St Joseph to be the most chaste spouse of the Blessed Virgin Mary and foster father to His Son Jesus Christ. St Joseph got to spend thirty years with Jesus, listening to His words of wisdom and witnessing on a personal level the perfect example of love and humility as Jesus obeyed and helped His foster father in all the household chores. How many of our great saints would also have had a great love and devotion to St Joseph for he has more power with God than any other saint, except the Blessed Virgin Mary, of course.

St Joseph was also privileged to have Jesus and the Blessed Virgin Mary present at his bedside as he died and as a result is patron saint of a happy death. St Joseph is also closely associated with the souls in purgatory and Holy Communion offered up to St Joseph for seven consecutive Sundays in honour of the Holy Souls is very pleasing to him. St Joseph witnessed all the personal trials and tribulations of family life and it is highly recommended to place your family, home, work etc under the patronage and protection of St Joseph on a daily basis.

St Joseph's Feast Day, 19th March, is the day prior to my father's date of death, 20th March and coincidentally, the Feast of Our Lady of the Rosary, 7th October, is the day prior to my mother's date of death, 8th October.

Our Guardian Angels

The public apparition of Our Lady in Medjugorje, for which Liz and myself were so privileged to be present, occurred on 2nd October, the feast day of our guardian angels. At the moment of our birth, God assigns to us our own personal guardian angel, who constantly remains by our side, protecting and guiding us as we travel on life's journey. It is highly recommended to call on your guardian angel to assist you in every situation you undertake, as otherwise they are compelled to stand back and honour the person's free will. We should therefore, upon awakening each morning, thank our guardian angel for keeping us safe throughout the night and ask him to accompany and protect us throughout the coming day. By doing this, each day may be spent in devotion and loving companionship with your own heavenly prince. Many of the saints had great devotion to their guardian angel and would always call on their assistance before undertaking any tasks.

The Passing of Two Great Men

Two very important and powerful men who both had a huge input into my recovery and spiritual awakening sadly passed away during my journey.

On Friday 6th April 2007, which happened to be Good Friday, my good and dear friend Fr Patsy Gallagher died. Fr Patsy Gallagher was ordained to the priesthood in 1950, and was our parish priest of Mevagh from 1979 to 2000. I was blessed to have known Fr Patsy, as he was such a powerful man. I will always remember our talk on 29th September 1993, and I will always be grateful for his blessings, prayers and words of wisdom. Fr Patsy Gallagher, thank you for everything. God bless.

I had the privilege of visiting Fr Willie Rafferty two months before he passed away; he was a patient in the hospital. He handed me two plastic bags that contained Rosaries, and blessed them from his hospital bed; he also gave me his special blessing. That evening, when I got home from work, I began to count and discovered fifty Rosaries in each bag. I felt so privileged and blessed to have been given so many Rosaries, and I knew then that Fr Willie Rafferty trusted me to share them with people who I should later meet on my travels.

On Monday 25th May 2009, I got the phone call informing me that our good friend Fr Willie Rafferty had passed away. Fr Willie

Rafferty and myself shared the same birthday – 3rd May – and the date of his death, 25th May, is the date of St Padre Pio's and my late father's birthday. I felt truly blessed to have met and known such a powerful man. Fr Willie Rafferty, thank you for everything. God bless.

Searching For My Roots

"They took it from the Jims," my father would say. My mother, meanwhile, would reply by saying, "We all know who the Jims are and where they came from, but nobody seems to know who or where your family came from".

That exchange of words between my late parents often intrigued me. I did remember my dad often talking about his two half brothers and sister, whom he never had the opportunity of meeting and Daddy always wondered whatever became of them.

I was also aware that, in 1964, my mother's brother James had disappeared without trace after leaving his lodgings in Glasgow where he was living at that time. I was sorry I didn't ask my parents more questions while they were both alive. Although it took me a total of fourteen years, I eventually got the answers about my long-lost aunt and uncles.

When my father's parents got married, they both had children from their previous marriages. My grandfather Edward's first wife died at a young age leaving him widowed with one son Denis, and my grandmother Sarah Ann's first husband also died young, leaving her a widow with two children, Mary Agnes and Patrick Joseph. After my grandparent's got married, they had two more sons, my uncle Edward and my father James. What was always a mystery was that their first children did not come with them into their second marriage.

After the sudden death of his mother, my uncle Denis McFadden was reared with his late mother's family relatives here in Donegal.

Denis would later emigrate to Philadelphia, and die tragically. On 30th October 1961 his body was recovered from the Schuylkill River, Philadelphia. Denis was a single man, aged 56, with no children that I'm aware off. My wife Liz and I travelled to his grave in Philadelphia, where I buried a little relic of St Anthony in his grave, which was my way of adding my own personal touch.

My search for my other uncle, Patrick Joseph Coyle, and his sister Mary Agnes proved to be much more difficult and complicated. After failing to locate any school records, etc. of them here in their native Donegal, I eventually discovered that, after the sudden death of their father, they were both placed into the care of Nazareth House Orphanage in Co Derry, Northern Ireland. I obtained a record of my aunt Mary Agnes entering Ellis Island, USA on 9th April 1920. It stated that Mary had 120 dollars in her possession, which was a huge amount of money back then.

I spent a lot of time then searching in the USA for possible records, without success. I eventually moved my search to London and as I couldn't locate any possible marriage certificate for my aunt, I continued searching using her maiden name and finally got a result. On 2nd February 1924, Mary Agnes, aged 26, was travelling by bus in London and, as she was alighting, she tripped and fell onto the pavement. Mary sustained fatal head injuries and died as a result. Mary was single with no children that I'm aware of.

I concentrated on finding the cemetery where Mary Agnes might be buried and, for some strange reason, I discovered my aunt was buried in a pauper's grave in St Patrick's cemetery, Leytonstone, London. Liz and I travelled to London and met with the cemetery superintendent. With his permission, we erected a cross in my aunt's memory, and I buried another relic of St Anthony underneath the cross. The cemetery has given me the opportunity to purchase this plot, so when this deal is finalised, I will be able to erect a little headstone which will be more permanent.

My search for my uncle Patrick Joseph took me back to the USA, to where I discovered he had moved and started a new life for himself. He met and married his wife Harriet and they had two daughters, Irene and Patricia. They lived in California where Patrick Joseph had started his own business. On 6th September 1941 the family were going on their holidays. Harriet was driving and, as she attempted to drive across a railway crossing, she saw the approaching train and applied the brakes, but the car swerved and crashed into the approaching Pacific Coast Railway train. Harriet died that same day due to the injuries she received. Patrick Joseph died the following January 27th 1942, also as a result of his injuries. Irene aged 9 and Patricia aged 5 both survived the accident but were also left orphans as a result.

Sometime after I discovered the tragic circumstances surrounding the deaths of Patrick Joseph and Harriet, I managed to trace my long lost cousin Patricia to her home in Chicago, where she and Irene were raised. Liz and myself visited Patricia, where we had a very special and emotional reunion and met up with our extended USA family cousins. Sadly, Irene died in 1995.

The successful outcome regarding my search for my Daddy's long lost sister and brothers gave me the courage and the inspiration not to give up hope in my search for my uncle James, as I was aware that my grandmother Sarah and several of my cousins had previously searched for James without success. I was also aware that there was no records whatsoever of James either alive or dead. I had a photograph of James, which was taken in my home in 1963 (year of my birth), during his last visit to our family.

After making extensive inquires, I followed up several possible sightings and rumours relating to his death, and travelled to Glasgow, London and Northampton, before finally concentrating my search in the Yorkshire area of England. During this research

I had made contact with two reliable sources, who told me they had met James in Doncaster and Leeds city centre respectively. Although they couldn't give a definite date, they both agreed it was around the years 1968-1970. One of my sources then suggested it was quite possible that James might have been using his mother's maiden name and, as a result, I finally discovered the sad and lonely downfall of my uncle James.

On the 28th December 1984, James, aged 58 passed away whilst a resident of Shaftesbury House Hostel, Beeston, Leeds. The cause of death was certified as cerebral haemorrhage. On presenting himself to the hostel, James would have been handed his room key, along with a set of bed clothing, and no request at that time would be made for a next of kin. I then discovered that, like my aunt Mary Agnes, James was also buried in a pauper's grave with six other poor souls who had lost all contact with family and loved ones.

Alcohol would have been the factor in my uncle James demise and his desire to remain anonymous and sever all links with his family at home bears the great sadness of one man's pride and darkness, which prevented him from reaching out and asking for the help and assistance that his family would have so much loved to pour out. When I was sharing the story of my family tree research with a friend they suggested that, as they all died so tragically I should have a Family Tree Healing Mass offered up.

For my 50th birthday I decided I would travel to Los Angeles, where Patrick Joseph and Harriet are buried. Prior to my trip I booked myself into a hotel and during my phone call, the lady looking after my reservation informed me the hotel I would be staying in was the hotel where everyone and anyone in Hollywood wanted to be seen.

My contact continued, "Mr McFadden, this is a real party hotel". I told my host I was really amused but I continued by adding, "Some short years ago I had a beautiful conversion and the purpose for this trip is to visit my long lost uncle's grave". I continued by adding, "my plan in life now is to save my soul and not to lose it". During our conversation, I stated my desire to attend Mass during my short trip to Los Angeles, so my contact sent me an e-mail with Mass times and addresses.

I had a most enjoyable and rewarding time in Los Angeles and got to visit and pray at Patrick Joseph and Harriet's grave. I also got to attend Mass in two separate churches, St Augustine's in Culver City and the Church of the Good Shepherd, Beverly Hills, both of which were within a short distance of my hotel. This once again proved to me the power of prayer, as my desire to go to Mass resulted in me meeting with some very caring and loving people who took me out to breakfast and dinner, as well as sightseeing in Beverly Hills, Hollywood etc. Rather than sample the nightlife that the hotel had to offer, I would go off for a walk around the surrounding area with my Rosary beads in my hand and pray the Rosary before retiring to my bed for the night.

My Devotion to the Holy Souls

During my search for my long lost family members, I prayed to my friend St Anthony, asking for his help as he is closely associated with lost souls. The eventual outcome of finding my relatives' graves and my most recent love and devotion to St Joseph, who is the patron saint of a happy death, started me off on a beautiful journey of self-discovery into what could be the outcome of my own soul when my time comes to face my judgment day.

When I shared these thoughts with my priest friend he suggested I do an examination of my conscience and take a note of any sins from my past that came into my mind. By doing this I realised and remembered many sins from my past that I had failed to mention or confess during my Confessions. Over a period of time, I took a note of any sin that came to my mind and when I did eventually think I had everything covered, I presented myself again to the beautiful Sacrament of Confession with my quite large list.

Although I had been attending Confession previously, I found that prior to my examination of conscience, there was quite a large number of sins that had yet to be addressed. This is something I would highly recommend to anyone who might find themselves in a situation similar to my own.

Fr Jose Maniyangat

I was carrying out my usual duties at work, collecting confidential papers for shredding and little did I know that when going to a particular bin, I would be taken on a most amazing journey that involved catching two separate flights and a trip that would take me 24 hours travelling to reach my destination.

As I was emptying the paper contents into my large clear bag, an A4 sheet of paper containing the testimony of Fr Jose Maniyangat just dropped into my hand. As I was about to throw it back into the bag, the headline 'Priest who experiences death is shown a vision of heaven, hell and purgatory' caught my eye. Without any hesitation I folded the paper and placed it inside my pocket.

After leaving the receptionist's office, I went into a nearby toilet, locked the door and started to read my precious find. What was interesting was that this same sheet of paper was taken from *Ireland's Eye* magazine, dated August 2009 which was five years previously. The nature and timing of this find amazed me. It proved how God was working His miracles and leading me to the text and material He wanted me to find as my spiritual journey was progressing.

When I got home from work, I went online and entered Fr Jose Maniyangat into the Google search engine and was pleased when I discovered Fr Jose was alive and well and now based as Pastor of 'St Catherine of Siena' church, Jacksonville, Florida. This same link also gave an e-mail address and once again I was overwhelmed when Fr Jose replied to my e-mail. Like me, Fr Jose was amazed how this came about. We exchanged several e-mails and phone calls and two months later I arrived in Jacksonville, Florida to meet in person this remarkable man of God.

Here is Fr Jose's personal testimony …

I was born on July 16th 1949 in Kerala, India to my parents, Joseph and Theresa Maniyangat. I am the eldest of seven children: Jose, Mary, Theresa, Lissama, Zachariah, Valsa and Tom. At the age of fourteen, I entered St Mary's minor seminary in Thiruvalla to begin my studies for the priesthood. Four years later I went to St Joseph's Pontifical Major Seminary in Alwaye, Kerala to continue my priestly formation. After completing the seven years of Philosophy and Theology I was ordained a priest on January 1st, 1975 to serve as a missionary at the Diocese of Thiruvalla. In 1978 while teaching at the St. Thomas minor seminary in St Mary's minor seminary in Bathery, I became an active member of the Charismatic Renewal movement and began conducting charismatic retreats and conferences in Kerala. On Sunday April 14th, 1985, the Feast of Divine Mercy, I was going to celebrate Mass at a mission church in the North part of Kerala, and I had a fatal accident. I was riding a motorcycle when I was hit head-on by a jeep driven by a man who was intoxicated after a Hindu festival. I was rushed to a hospital about 35 miles away. On the way my soul came out from my body and I experienced death. Immediately I met my Guardian Angel. I saw my body and the people who were carrying me to the hospital. I heard them crying and praying for me. At this time my Angel told me: "I am going to take you to Heaven, the Lord wants to meet you and talk with you" He also said that on the way he wanted to show me hell and purgatory.

First, the angel escorted me to hell. It was an awful sight! I saw Satan and the devils, an unquenchable fire of about 2,000

Fahrenheit degrees, worms crawling, people screaming and fighting, others being tortured by demons. The angel told me that all these sufferings were due to unrepented mortal sins. Then, I understood that there are seven degrees of sufferings or levels according to the number and kinds of mortal sins committed in their earthly lives. The souls looked very ugly, cruel and horrific. It was a fearful experience. I saw people whom I knew but I am not allowed to reveal their identities. The sins that convicted them were mainly abortion, homosexuality, euthanasia, hatefulness, unforgiveness and sacrilege. The angel told me that if they had repented they would have avoided hell and gone instead to purgatory. I also understood that some people who repent from these sins might be purified on earth through their sufferings. This way they can avoid purgatory and go straight to heaven.

I was surprised when I saw in hell even Priests and Bishops, some of whom I never expected to see. Many of them were there because they mislead the people with false teachings and bad example.

After the visit to hell, my Guardian angel escorted me to purgatory. Here too, there are seven degrees of sufferings and unquenchable fire. But it is far less intense than hell and there was neither quarrelling nor fighting. The main suffering of these souls is their separation from God. Some of those who are in purgatory committed numerous mortal sins, but they were reconciled with God before their death. Even though these souls are suffering, they enjoy peace and the knowledge that one day they will see God face to face.

I had a chance to communicate with the souls in purgatory. They asked me to pray for them and to tell the people to pray for them as well, so they can go to heaven quickly.

When we pray for these souls we will receive their gratitude through their prayers and once they enter heaven their prayers become even more meritorious.

It is difficult for me to describe how beautiful my Guardian angel is. He is radiant and bright. He is my constant companion and helps me in all my ministries, especially my healing ministry. I experience his presence everywhere I go and I am grateful for his protection in my daily life.

Next my angel escorted me to heaven passing through a big dazzling white tunnel. I never experienced this much peace and joy in my life. Then immediately the heaven opened up and I heard the most delightful music, which I never heard before. The angels were singing and praising God. I saw all the saints, especially the Blessed Mother and St Joseph, and many dedicated holy Bishops and Priests who were shining like stars. And when I appeared before the Lord, Jesus told me: "I want you to go back to the world. In your second life you will be an instrument of peace and healing to my people. You will walk in a foreign land and you will speak in a foreign tongue. Everything is possible for you with my grace". After these words, the Blessed Mother told me: "Do whatever He tells you. I will help you in all your ministries".

Words can not express the beauty of heaven. There we find so much peace and happiness, which exceeds a million times our imagination. Our Lord is far more beautiful than any image can convey. His face is radiant and luminous and more beautiful than a thousand rising suns. The pictures we see in the world are only a shadow of His magnificence. The Blessed Mother was next to Jesus: she was so beautiful and radiant. None of the images we see in this world can compare with her real beauty. Heaven is our real home, we are all created to reach heaven and enjoy God forever. Then, I came back to the world with my angel.

While my body was at the hospital, the doctor completed all examinations and I was pronounced dead. The cause of death was bleeding. My family was notified and since they were far away, the hospital staff decided to move my dead body to the morgue. Because the hospital did not have air conditioners they were concerned that the body would decompose quickly. As they were moving my dead body to the morgue, my soul came back to the body. I felt an excruciating pain because of so many wounds and broken bones. I began to scream and then the people became frightened and ran away screaming. One of them approached the doctor and said: "the dead body is screaming". The doctor came to examine the body and found that I was alive. So he said: "Father is alive, it is a miracle, take him back to the hospital".

Now, back at the hospital, they gave me blood transfusions and I was taken to surgery to repair the broken bones. They worked on my lower jaw, ribs, pelvic bone, wrists, and right leg. After two months, I was released from the hospital, but my orthopaedic doctor said that I would never walk again. I said to him: "the Lord who gave me my life back and sent me back to the world will heal me". Once at home we were all praying for a miracle. Still after a month and with the casts removed I was not able to move. But one day while praying I felt an extraordinary pain in my pelvic area. After a short while the pain disappeared completely and I heard a voice saying: "you are healed. Get up and walk". I felt the peace and healing power on my body. I immediately got up and walked. I praised and thanked God for the miracle. I reached my doctor with the news of my healing and he was amazed. He said: "your

God is the true God. I must follow your God". The doctor was Hindu and he asked me to teach him about our Church. After studying the faith, I baptized him and he became Catholic.

Following the message from my Guardian Angel, I came to the United States on November 10, 1986 as a missionary Priest. First, I worked in the Diocese of Boise, Idaho from 1987 to 1989 and then became the Director of Prison Ministry in the Diocese of Orlando, Florida from 1989 to 1992. In 1992, I came to the Diocese of St Augustine where I was first assigned to St Matthew's Parish in Jacksonville for two years. I was then appointed Parochial Vicar of Assumption Church from 1994 to 1999. In 1997 I was incardinated as a permanent member of the Diocese. From June 1999 to June 2011, I was Pastor of St Mary's Mother of Mercy Catholic Church in Macclenny, Florida. I also served as the Catholic Chaplain for Florida State Prison in Starke, Union Correctional Institution in Raiford and Northeast Florida State Hospital in Macclenny. On July 1, 2011 I was assigned to St Catherine of Siena Catholic Church in Orange Park, Florida. I am also the Diocesan Spiritual Director of the Legion of Mary.

On the first Saturday of each month I conduct a Eucharistic and charismatic-healing ministry at my current parish St Catherine of Siena Catholic Church in Orange Park, Florida. People come from all over the diocese, many parts of Florida and even from out of the state. I have been invited to conduct the healing ministry in other major cities of the United States including: New York, Philadelphia, Washington DC, San Jose, Dallas, Chicago, Birmingham, Denver, Boise, Idaho Falls, Hawaii, Miami, Ft. Lauderdale, Poolsville; and many other countries: Ireland, Spain, Czech Republic, India, France, Portugal, Yugoslavia, Italy, Canada, Mexico, Cayman Island, and Ontario.

Through this Eucharistic-healing ministry I have seen many people healed physically, spiritually, mentally and emotionally. People with various illnesses such as: cancer, AIDs, arthritis, heart conditions, eye problems, emphysema, asthma, back pains, bad hearing and many others have been healed completely. In addition, several times during the year I conduct a special healing service for the healing of the family tree, in which the effects from ancestral sins are blocked and the person receives complete healing. Scripture says that the effects from family sins can linger around for three to five generations (Exodus Chapter 34 verse 7). So, in many cases we need generational healing. Doctors and medicines do not help to heal certain sickness caused by our family tree.

During the Healing ministry, many people rest in the spirit before the Blessed Sacrament and some experience renewal of the soul and healing of the body.

During my meeting with Fr Jose, I was pleased to discover that St Alphonsa of India, canonised in 2008 by Pope Benedict XVI is an aunt of Fr Jose.

Church Dedicated to the Holy Souls in Purgatory

The Church of the Sacred Heart of Suffrage, Rome (Chiesa del Sacro Cuore del Suffragio) contains a number of relics/photographic evidence of various objects bearing visible, physical marks left by souls in purgatory. These marks were left when the soul returned seeking and asking for Masses and prayers to release them. These relics/photographs are displayed inside a glass unit on the wall of a room in the Sacristy area of the Church. The collection is known as the Piccolo Museo Del Purgatorio (Little Museum of Purgatory).

During a visit to Rome, Liz and myself had the privilege of being present for Mass in this very special church and witness on a personal level the relics/photographs of the Holy Souls in purgatory. This same church is a short ten-minute walk from the Vatican and I would highly recommend paying it a visit should you find yourself in Rome.

Two Popes, Pope Pius X and Pope Benedict XV have approved this church.

* * * * * * *

During that same trip to Rome, Liz and myself had the privilege of being present for a public audience and blessing from Pope Francis. This was really special and personal to us both as during a previous visit to Rome we had obtained the same privilege from Pope Benedict XVI and Saint John Paul II, during his papacy, had bestowed his apostolic blessing on the occasion of our marriage.

St Faustina's Vision of Hell

On 30th April 2000 Pope John Paul II canonised St Faustina.

St Faustina was born Helena Kowalska on 25th August 1905 in the village of Glogowiec, Poland. When she was twenty years old, she entered the apostolic congregation of the Sisters of Our Lady of Mercy, where as a humble and hardworking sister, she lived the final thirteen years of her short life. St Faustina died on 5th October 1938, in the convent of her congregation at Lagiewniki in Cracow, Poland.

In 1936, Sister Faustina was shown a vision of hell.

Here is an account taken from her Diary (741).

"Today, I was led by an angel to the chasms of hell. It is a place of great torture; how awesomely large and extensive it is! The kinds of tortures I saw: the first torture that constitutes hell is the loss of God; the second is perpetual remorse of conscience; the third is that one's condition will never change; (160) the fourth is the fire that will penetrate the soul without destroying it – a terrible suffering, since it is a purely spiritual fire, lit by God's anger; the fifth torture is continual darkness and a terrible suffocating smell, and, despite the darkness, the devils and the souls of the damned see each other and all the evil, both of others and their own; the sixth torture is the constant company of Satan; the seventh torture is the horrible despair, hatred of God, vile words, curses and blasphemies. These are the tortures suffered by all the damned together, but that is not the end of the sufferings. There are special tortures destined for particular souls. These are the torments of the senses. Each soul undergoes terrible and indescribable sufferings, related to the manner in which it has sinned. There are caverns and pits of torture where one form of agony differs from another. I would have died at the very sight of these tortures if the omnipotence of God had not supported me. Let the sinner know that he will be tortured throughout all eternity, in those senses which he made use of to sin. (161) I am writing this at the command of God, so that no soul may find an excuse by saying there is no hell, or that nobody has ever been there, and so no one can say what it is like. I, Sister Faustina, by the order of God, have visited the abysses of hell so that I might tell souls about it and testify to its existence. I cannot speak about it now; but I have received a command from God to leave it in writing. The devils were full of hatred for me, but they had to obey me at the command of God. What I have written is but a pale shadow of the things I saw. But I noticed one thing: that most of the souls there are those who disbelieved that there is a hell. When I came to, I could hardly recover from the fright. How terribly souls suffer there! Consequently, I pray even more fervently for the conversion of sinners. I incessantly plead God's mercy upon them. O my Jesus, I would rather be in agony until the end of the world, amidst the greatest sufferings, than offend You by the least sin."

The Chaplet of Divine Mercy

Our Lord revealed to Sister Faustina, the Chaplet of Divine Mercy, a powerful prayer that He wanted her to pray, and the Lord urged her to encourage others to say it too and make it known to the whole world, promising extraordinary graces to those who would recite this special prayer.

Our Lord said to Sister Faustina:
> Encourage souls to say the Chaplet which I have given you ... Whoever will recite it will receive great mercy at the hour of death ... When they say this Chaplet in the presence of the dying, I will stand between My Father and the dying person, not as the just judge but as the Merciful Saviour ... Priests will recommend it to sinners as their last hope of salvation. Even if there were a sinner most hardened, if he were to recite this Chaplet only once, he would receive grace from My infinite mercy ... Through the Chaplet you will obtain everything, if what you ask for is compatible with My will.
>
> Like the Rosary, I have also included the Chaplet of Divine Mercy in my daily prayers.

Our Lord also instructed Sister Faustina to have the Image of Divine Mercy painted and venerated throughout the whole world. The Divine Mercy image first appeared to Sister Faustina in her room on 22nd February 1931.

"In the evening in my cell, I saw Jesus clothed in white, one hand raised in blessing, the other resting on His breast. From His garment came rays of light, one red and the other pale in colour. Jesus said to me, "Paint an image according to the vision you see, with the signature "Jesus I trust in You". I desire that this image be venerated first in your chapel and then throughout the world. The two beams of light shining forth from My Heart are the symbols of blood and water that poured from My side on the day of My Sacrifice on Calvary. The pale beam represents the water that cleanses and purifies souls, the red, the blood that gives new life to souls".

The correct Divine Mercy image should have the words "Jesus I trust in You" inscribed under, and not on the image. Our Lord also promised extraordinary graces to all who venerate this Image and after I first became aware of this very special devotion, I was inspired to obtain this beautiful Image and have it placed in our home.

Taking Stock of My Life

As I reflect on my life and my journey to date, I am fully aware there can be no turning back to my old ways. Although I still get the odd mad notion occasionally, I try and put it out of my mind immediately and replace it with a prayer or an act of charity. Before I would dwell on these crazy thoughts, and nine times out of ten I would go about trying to act them out.

I know I will always have my demons attacking me, and it is no coincidence that alcohol is also known by the name spirits and those same spirits could quite easily be described as evil spirits. You only have to look at the statistics to see the devastation that alcohol abuse is causing on a worldwide scale. For me, personally, there is no doubt that the devil is in the bottle. The only way to beat the devil is through prayer and I get great comfort from the fact that nothing can overcome the power of prayer.

I remember one time, during the Sacrament of Reconciliation, I confessed that my mind kept wandering as I was trying to say my prayers. The priest gave me this simple but very effective advice, "When you are talking about someone, or talking to someone you know on the phone, you will have a mental image of that person in your mind's eye. So too when you are saying your prayers, get an image of the person whom you are praying too and just imagine you are talking personally one-to-one with that person".

I'm still employed as a porter in Letterkenny General Hospital, where my job brings me into contact on a daily basis with patients, concerned family members etc, and it's good to get the chance to offer some words of comfort and hope and to share my own personal experience and testimony.

God has a plan for each and every one of us, so our goal in this life should be to discover this plan and become the saints that God truly desires us to be. We all like to have a goal, but to try and achieve your goal, you need a plan, as a goal without a plan is just a dream. It's also very important to think positively, as negative thoughts will only bring you down. When you set your sights on a certain goal, I think it's very important to be prepared for the long struggle ahead. Determination and perseverance can eventually get you a result, and quite possibly the success you once imagined achieving.

Determination and perseverance are also required when you are praying or making a novena asking God for a favour. If your prayer is not answered the first time, or within the time period promised with the certain novena, then don't give up hope; just continue on praying and keep on asking. If what you are asking for is according to God's will, then God will grant it when the time is right. If what you are praying for is not according to the will of God, then God will grant you something else which will be equally or even more beneficial to your needs.

It is never too late to turn one's life around. One only has to look at the life and example of the great St Augustine, who lived a life of sin and debauchery before he finally realised the error of his ways. He even fathered a child out of wedlock. St Augustine's mother St Monica prayed for many many years for her wayward son to change his ways and her prayer was finally answered with the most beautiful conversion of St Augustine. I have no doubt that my own parents never gave up hope as they both prayed faithfully for the conversion and sobriety of their own wayward son.

I'm also very aware how blessed I was that Liz and St Anthony both had good patience with me while I was on that wrong path and a very dangerous journey, during my years of alcoholic binges, selfish and sinful lifestyle. I thank God for sparing me during that dark, lonely and painful existence.

Women can also take great comfort and hope from the testimony of Dorothy Day, an American lady who died as recently as 1980. Before her own beautiful conversion, Dorothy Day lived a party lifestyle and even had an abortion, an act which she deeply regretted. In March 2000 Pope John Paul II granted the Archdiocese of New York in which she lived, permission to open her cause for beatification and canonisation, allowing her to be called a Servant of God in the eyes of the Catholic Church. Once again, this proves the mercy and love of God once we renounce our sins and ask for His forgiveness.

During my travels, it's not unusual for me to be seen sitting on a bus, train, plane, in an airport, or maybe walking on a beach with my Rosary beads in my hand reciting my prayers. When I visited Lourdes, I bought a small statue of the Infant Jesus of Prague, in Medjugorje I was presented with a small statue of St Anthony and the Baby Jesus and I purchased a beautiful small picture of the Holy Family in a charity shop in my native Letterkenny. I have placed these in my rucksack/hand luggage, wrapped and protected in bubble wrap, so wherever my travels might take me, I place these along with my prayer books on my bedside locker to say my night and morning prayers. For my added protection and peace of mind, I have sewn together the green and brown scapular, with the miraculous medal placed inside. I wear these blessed devotional objects around my neck.

Another great example of the power of prayer in achieving and maintaining sobriety can be found in the testimony of the Venerable Matt Talbot.

Matt Talbot was born in Dublin on 2nd May 1856 and died on 7th June 1925 on his way to Mass. In his early teenage years, Matt became an alcoholic, but at the age of twenty-eight he took the pledge and managed to remain sober for the next forty-one years of his life. Matt devoted his life of sobriety to prayer, penance and great acts of charity.

Pope Paul VI declared him 'Venerable' on 3rd October 1975 and he only requires two miracles for beatification. I would also highly recommend anyone suffering from an addiction to pray to the Venerable Matt Talbot and seek his intercession. By doing so, one will be helping themselves and also the eventual canonisation of this remarkable man. The tomb of the Venerable Matt Talbot is located in Our Lady of Lourdes church, Sean McDermott Street, Dublin.

Like the Venerable Matt Talbot, I am happy and confident to leave my sobriety in the hands of God and the power of prayer each day. "Alcoholics Anonymous" has helped multitudes of people worldwide achieve sobriety, but AA alone will not save your soul.

Where would I be today without prayer … I have no doubt that I would be in my grave and my loved ones praying for my soul.

Printed in Great Britain
by Amazon